IMI *information service*
Sandyford, Dublin 16
Telephone 2078513 Fax 295 9479
email library@imi.ie
Internet http://www.imi.ie

Consumer Research and Policy Series
Edited by Gordon Foxall

Consumer Psychology in Behavioural Perspective
Gordon Foxall

Morality and the Market
Consumer pressure for corporate accountability
N. Craig Smith

Innovation and the Network
Wim G. Biemans

Consumer Profiles
An Introduction to Psychographics
Barrie Gunter and Adrian Furnham

Consumer Behaviour in China
Customer Satisfaction and Cultural Values
Oliver Yau

Professional Purchasing

Lars-Erik Gadde and
Håkan Håkansson

London and New York

First published 1993
by Routledge
11 New Fetter Lane, London EC4P 4EE

First published in paperback 1994

Simultaneously published in the USA and Canada
by Routledge
29 West 35th Street, New York, NY 10001

© 1993 Lars-Erik Gadde and Håkan Håkansson

Typeset in Times by J&L Composition Ltd, Filey, North Yorkshire
Printed and bound in Great Britain by
Mackays of Chatham PLC, Chatham, Kent

British Library Cataloguing in Publication Data
A catalogue record for this book is available
from the British Library.

Library of Congress Cataloging-in-Publication Data
has been applied for.

ISBN 0–415–10397–5 (pbk)

Contents

Figures and tables

FIGURES

TABLES

Foreword

This book is about the benefits of building up close supplier relationships and connecting them into efficient supplier networks. Looking back at the process leading to this book, we have to admit that the theme of the book also can be identified in our way of working. We have had the luck and pleasure to work closely with researchers and practitioners, who in different ways have contributed to the final product. Some of them have provided constructive criticism regarding both the content and the form. Others have given illustrations or suggested managerial implications and others have had ideas regarding the development of the theoretical framework which the work is built on. All the contributors cannot be named, but we will mention the most important ones.

At Uppsala University, the Department of Business Studies, we would like to express our gratitude to Ann-Kristin Eriksson, Maria Åsberg, Barbara Henders, Björn Axelsson, Jens-Laage Hellman, Alexandra Waluszewski, Ivan Snehota and Jan Johanson. At Chalmers University of Technology we would in the same way thank Anna Dubois, Ragnar Hörndahl and Hans Björnsson.

The book is building on and utilizing earlier studies and publications about purchasing where we have benefited from the co-operation with Björn Wootz (now at NCC), Björn Axelsson, Uppsala University, and Leif Melin, Linköping University. Other important strategic alliances have been with Lars-Gunnar Mattsson and Anders Lundgren at the Stockholm School of Economics.

We also have had the good fortune to be part of the IMP co-operation. Parts of the book have been discussed at the IMP conferences and we have received valuable comments and suggestions from, among others, David Ford, University of Bath, Peter W. Turnbull and Malcolm Cunningham, UMIST, Jean-Paul Valla and Robert Spencer, IRE, Lyon, Dave Wilson, Penn State University, Geoff Easton and Luis Araujo, University of Lancaster, and Phil Smith, University of Hull. A part of the book was written when one of the authors was visiting professor at the Marketing Department, Kellogg Graduate School of Management, Northwestern University. The seminars and discussions regarding relationships and networks with James Anderson, Dawn Iacobucci, Philip Kotler, Louis Stern and Phil Zarillo have been highly appreciated and an important input to this book.

The book is summarizing our experience over a twenty-year period where we have had the opportunity to work together with a number of managers in different companies. We would like to especially mention Erik Asplund and Mikael Öberg, SIAB, Björn Wallin, NCC, Lars-Eric Olson, Kommentusgruppen, Per Bexelius, Mitera, Håkan Fröling, Stockholm Energi, Hans Barkman, Samhall, Ulf Carresjö, SKF, Christer Cederblad, Skanska, Seth Jonsson, Inköpsledarna, Bengt Rehnberg, Kommunförbundet, Sven-Erik Håkansson, Essex, Ola Nilsson, Thorsman, Lars-Uno Roos, Volvo, Ingela Björk-Loch, Solectron, Hans Werner, Nordwin, Pär Aspengren, ASG, Hans-Åke Norås, Leksells, Kent Edvinsson, Atlet, Odd Jacobsen and Roland Eriksson, Järnia, and a large number of participants of the executive master program at Uppsala University. An important network node during the process has been Göran Liljegren and the organization he leads, Marketing Technology Center, in Stockholm.

We also express our gratitude to Marita Ahlkvist and Inger Håkansson, who typed the manuscript, and Linda Schenk, who made the translation to English.

Last, but not least, we gratefully acknowledge the economic resources provided by Axel och Margaret Ax:son Johnsons stiftelse för allmännyttiga ändamål, NUTEK and the research programme Information Technology and Management, conducted by the Institute for Management of Innovation and Technology.

Uppsala and Gothenburg, September 1992
Lars-Erik Gadde
Håkan Håkansson

Chapter 1

Purchasing – a function of growing importance

By virtue of the grace invested in my royal office I have decreed unto you to forge one thousand suits of armour and ten thousand arrowheads.

You have failed to obey this command!

At the peril of having your heads fall to the axe, to the amusement of the inhabitants of Stockholm, in the city square one holiday eve at my discretion, I once again command you to comply with my wishes.

Gustavus Vasa, King of Sweden, issued this decree in the sixteenth century to the Kungshammaren crown foundry. It is the earliest example we have found of the way a purchaser sees and deals with his suppliers, and provides us with a point of departure for discussing our motivation in writing the present book.

First and foremost, in many companies purchasing is a changing function. Both the view of the importance of purchasing and purchasing methods are changing and, consequently, so are relations to suppliers. The growing importance of purchasing is a result of the increasing specialization which characterizes the industrial system as a whole. Companies have gradually concentrated their activities more and more on parts of the total production chain. A company usually consists of several production units. The tendency towards specialization is particularly notable at this level of the industrial system. Individual production units have become more and more specialized over time. However, as the demands from the ultimate market are not correspondingly segmented, companies that have limited their own operations tend to use external specialists to offer their customers a package solution. In this way, external suppliers have gained importance in relation to manufacturing companies, at which purchased goods often account for more than 50 per cent of the total turnover.

One result of this is that what goes on at the interface between individual companies has gradually gained in importance in relation to the effectiveness and development of industrial systems. Concepts and techniques such as 'just in time' (JIT) deliveries, the zero-defect principle and quality assurance have more and more impact on company operations. All of this means bringing the relationships between a firm and its suppliers into focus, as well as the greater significance of the purchasing function.

One natural consequence of all this is that the competitiveness and profit-generating capacity of the individual firm is highly dependent on its ability to handle purchasing. Initially, there is a direct effect on profitability, as purchasing accounts for a substantial portion of company costs. Secondly, there is an indirect impact, because 'internal costs' are greatly affected by what goes on at the interface between individual companies and their suppliers.

This background makes it easy to understand companies which see effective purchasing as a vital element in competition, with major strategic impact. Gustavus Vasa himself undoubtedly realized its importance. A secure supply of arrowheads and suits of armour was decisive to the competitive power of the royal kingdom of Sweden.

Let us then consider King Gustavus's purchasing behaviour. His letter indicates that the supplier, the Kungshammaren crown foundry did not comply with the commitments conferred upon it by His Majesty's royal grace. The powerful purchaser reacted not only by threatening to cancel the business transaction in question but also by threatening to make all future business impossible. This type of behaviour appears peculiar in light of the fact that this was a piece of business relating to a strategic item for the buyer. It can, of course, be explained by saying that the king had access to a large number of potential alternative suppliers. There was no decisive difference between their products, nor did the products require substantial adaptation to the process in which they were to be used by the buyer. In this respect, the behaviour of King Gustavus may be viewed as rational, as long as he refrained from decapitating all his potential suppliers. The purchasing strategy of the king put pressure on his suppliers to do their utmost. (A note on terminology: The term 'purchaser' is used for a person working with purchasing. By 'buyer' we mean the company active in procurement, sometimes also referred to as the purchasing company or the buying company. On the supply side we use the terms 'supplier', 'vendor' and 'seller' as interchangeable terms for the supplying company.)

The purchasing strategy of Gustavus Vasa was widely emulated during the following four centuries. Putting pressure on individual suppliers and playing them off against one another to attain lower prices has been the prevailing philosophy. The means available to the purchasing companies have not always been as forceful as Gustavus Vasa's, but in many cases major buyers have very powerful positions in relation to their small subcontractors. Today, too, many purchasing operations are carried out in the spirit of King Gustavus Vasa.

However, the prerequisites for corporate purchasing have changed over time. There have been drastic changes in the number and size distribution of alternative suppliers available. This is true not only in relation to military procurement, but for all markets. The interchangeability of suppliers has also decreased. This is the result of greater dependence between customer and supplier, owing to increased specialization. Efficiency improvements from JIT supplies and quality assurance require the active involvement of both parties. Co-operation between customer and supplier over an extended period of time with successive identification of potential improvements has also become a necessity. In this situation we must question the method of dealing with suppliers launched by Gustavus Vasa, henceforth referred to as the traditional model.

In the last twenty years, a new view of purchasing has developed at many companies. This book analyses the changing role of purchasing. It is our ambition to apply the new insights concerning the increased importance of purchasing to different aspects of purchasing work. Our theme throughout is that professional purchasing work should focus on constant improvement of the coupling between one's own firm and its suppliers. There is really no ultimate limit to these efforts; effectiveness will always be open to improvement through interaction with suppliers. It is important to emphasize that this increased collaboration does not mean placing fewer demands on one's suppliers. On the contrary, in most cases demands increase. We analyse the factors which affect – i.e. worsen or facilitate – this teamwork. We also discuss what characterizes professional purchasing work according to the new model for purchasing we have identified in this book.

Chapter 1 discusses the significance of purchasing in detail, and the respects in which purchasing may be seen as a strategic function.

THE IMPORTANCE OF PURCHASING

We have already pointed out that purchasing accounts for a substantial portion of the total costs of a firm. In a study of four large assembling firms in the mechanical engineering industry, the average share was found to be 65 per cent (Grant 1990). The changes between 1976 and 1987 for a large engineering firm can be illustrated as follows. The costs of the firm can be divided into three main groups: personnel salaries, purchased goods and miscellaneous costs. For both years, miscellaneous costs were 20 per cent of the total costs, while there was a dramatic change in the proportions of the other two cost items. In 1976, salaries accounted for 43 per cent and purchased goods for 37 per cent. In 1987 this relationship had reversed, and purchasing accounted for 60 per cent of total costs, while personnel salaries accounted for 20 per cent.

In smaller companies, too, purchasing often accounts for a large proportion of costs, as can be seen in Table 1.1, where data from a study of 123 small and medium-sized Swedish companies are reported.

We find that in every fourth company, purchasing accounted for more than 60 per cent of total turnover. In nearly half of the

Table 1.1 Portion of firm's turnover accounted for by purchasing

Portion of turnover for purchasing %	Proportion of companies %
0–24	7
25–39	22
40–49	30
50–59	16
60–79	19
80–100	6

Source: Håkansson 1989: 76

companies (46 per cent), it accounted for between 40 and 60 per cent. About 30 per cent of the companies stated that purchasing accounted for less than 40 per cent. This should imply that for no fewer than seven out of every ten companies, purchasing was the main expenditure. There is only a limited amount of data available with regard to observations of developments over time. From it, we conclude that the proportion has increased over time (see Gadde 1989). In other words, companies decide more and more frequently to make use of external suppliers. This applies both to production and to development work. The same tendency appears to apply to purchasing in the public sector.

The increasing proportion of purchasing is a consequence of increased specialization. Looking forward, we see no reason to believe that this trend will break. The more highly developed society becomes, the greater the degree of differentiation, and the more specialized units we can anticipate. As a result of this increased proportion of purchasing, purchasing itself has come to be successively involved in an increasingly large fraction of a company's total operations. This means that the capacity and competence of the purchasing department will be important to the effectiveness of the firm.

Therefore, owing to its already large volume, purchasing is an essential aspect of the profitability of a firm. Another reason for its increased importance is that purchasing also has a direct impact on revenues. If we presume that all other variables remain unchanged, every pound saved on purchasing is a pound of profit. Unfortunately, far too many managers confuse this idea with the notion that a pound off the price is also a pound of profit. Nothing could be further from the truth, as many managers who have tried to reduce purchasing costs by overly stereotyped means have soon realized. The explanation for this confusion is to be found in the indirect costs associated with purchasing. What happens is that defects or other problems with purchased products lead either to major production costs, demands for service or customer complaints. The purchased goods or services must then not be seen in isolation, but rather in relation to the function they are meant to fulfil. Moreover, they also have to be handled administratively, commercially, technically and/or physically, and this is also associated with numerous costs. One example is tied-up capital and the costs related to storage of purchased materials and components. The design of purchased goods and services also affects the firm's production and development. A firm may increase the efficiency of its own production by purchasing pre-processed materials and well-designed components. There are examples where co-operation with a supplier has reduced the number of components required by half, which of course has an effect in the form of direct cost reductions in the firm's production process. Similarly, a firm can affect both costs and the necessity of in-house development work by co-ordinating its efforts with those of the various suppliers. As is described and analysed further on, total indirect costs are often of great magnitude. For individual products or types of products they may be as significant as the price. In other words, means of purchasing affects a number of other costs besides the direct purchasing price.

A third factor which has meant an increase in the importance of purchasing is the realization of the benefits to be reaped from deeper more long-term co-operation with a supplier. Examples include materials flows (JIT deliveries), information flow (computerized communication) or collaboration on technical development. Some companies which are highly dependent on purchasing now have an explicit policy of extended co-operation with their suppliers. For example, the external purchasing policy issued by the passenger-car division at Saab states that Saab considers its suppliers to be an integral part of the total Saab production system. The policy goes on to state that openness, mutual trust, and long-term undertakings result in profitability for both parties involved. This type of attitude, also indicated in the policies of other automobile manufacturers, reflects a major change in purchasing behaviour, which was previously characterized in terms such as 'price has been the principal yardstick' (Dillforce 1986: 13).

A fourth factor showing the increased importance of purchasing is the greater complexity of the purchasing function. Owing to specialization, the products purchased today are more sophisticated and have more technological content, making the task of purchasing more difficult. Complexity has also risen in step with the proportion of international purchases. This has led both to increased distance to suppliers and the problems arising with this, as well as additional problems relating to currencies, exchange rates and local legislation.

THE ROLE OF THE PURCHASING FUNCTION

The section above has demonstrated that purchasing and purchasing behaviour have substantial effects on company revenues. It became increasingly clear during the 1980s that purchasing may be crucial to the competitiveness of a firm. This view has been asserted in both Swedish and American literature (Axelsson and Håkansson 1984, Spekman 1988). We use the terminology of Axelsson and Håkansson (1984) to give a comprehensive view of the potential of purchasing to affect a company's strategic competition status. They distinguish three strategic roles in purchasing: the rationalization role, the developmental role and the structural role.

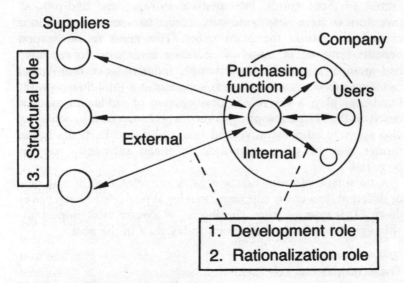

Figure 1.1 The roles of purchasing

The rationalization role

The rationalization role of purchasing comprises all the day-to-day activities performed to decrease costs successively. This may include improving or reducing the costs associated with various flows, or finding new solutions to technical or other problems. Three main types of rationalization activities may be identified.

The first type is related to discovering what needs to be purchased. This includes decisions on whether to purchase or manufacture in-house, as well as the design of the products/ components which are to be purchased. It is possible for purchasing to contribute to an increase in effectiveness through co-operation with internal functions such as design, development and production, and through good awareness of what different suppliers have to offer. One method which is often mentioned, but more seldom applied, is known as value analysis. Value analysis is an attempt to systematize a review of the value of various functions of a given product or solution, and to find alternative ways of satisfying the corresponding functions.

Rationalization of flows comprises the second aspect of effectiveness. Material flow, for example, was often focused on during the 1980s. Capital efficiency measures and reduction of inventories (stores of input goods, intermediate storage, and end-product inventories) have also gradually come to include operations carried on outside the plant gates. The great rationalization benefits achieved in terms of reducing inventory storage have had multiple effects for the assembly industry since they began including subcontractors and their suppliers in a total flow concept. Purchasing plays a key role in development of production systems based on the JIT philosophy. Moreover, effectiveness benefits can also apply to administrative and financial flows. Particularly the former may be of a magnitude to mean substantial savings potential.

A third type of rationalization gains are related to finding new or different, less costly suppliers, making it possible to keep prices down. This type of price chasing is, of course, still important, although it may be less dominant today than in the past.

The developmental role

For a purchasing firm, suppliers are an important potential development resource. In many cases they are only used passively, i.e. the purchasing company waits for the supplier to develop new solutions and then decides whether or not to purchase them. Active work, however, can turn the purchasing function into a major catalyst for taking better advantage of this resource. We refer to this as the developmental role of purchasing.

There are numerous good reasons for a purchasing firm to become involved in the development work of its suppliers, and also to interest the suppliers in becoming involved in the purchasing firm's development work. One is that better co-ordination is achieved in comparison with each one going forward along its own lines: the products developed are already familiar to the user. A second advantage is related to the increased developmental power that can be obtained from interaction of different resources. A third advantage is that time is saved – working in parallel instead of in series may lead to major time benefits in development work.

All in all, many factors speak in favour of closer co-operation as beneficial to both customer and supplier.

We can see that the need for collaboration in development, and the consequent significance of the developmental role of purchasing, has increased over time. One reason is the fragmentation and increased specialization of the production system. A purchasing firm which uses components from different areas of technology will, of course, find it difficult to develop and maintain its own knowledge of all these special fields. In such cases it is natural for them to try to make use of the developmental resources of their suppliers. Another reason is the need to try to shorten lead times for design and development. This is considered one of the most important competitive factors in many industries today. To accomplish this, development work between customer and supplier must be better co-ordinated.

The structural role

The structural role of the purchasing function is defined as the way in which companies affect the structure of the supplier markets. A company may choose to concentrate its purchases with one supplier. This strengthens the competitiveness of that supplier in relation to others. Alternately, the purchasing firm may choose the strategy of dividing its purchases among suppliers in order to contribute to the maintenance of a number of alternative means of supply. Analogously, geographical location may be a decisive factor in choice of supplier. The firm may want to have its main suppliers close at hand in order to have the prerequisites for co-operation and development potential. Alternately, the firm may choose to use suppliers located at important centres of technology. This gives the firm a channel to the forefront of developments.

The conscious and unconscious actions of the purchasing firm affect the structure of the purchasing market in terms of the long-range numbers and locations of the alternative suppliers. For this reason, it is important for a company to analyse the long-term consequences of its purchasing behaviour. It is equally important for a purchasing firm to successively identify other trends in structural development in relation to its main supplier markets. This makes it possible for the firm to orientate its own operations towards reinforcing the tendencies beneficial to it and counteracting undesirable ones.

THE OBJECTIVES AND APPROACHES OF THIS BOOK

This book aims to analyse the new view of company purchasing which has gradually developed. One consequence of the increasing importance of issues relating to purchasing is that ideas about purchasing and what characterizes efficient purchasing have been reviewed. Price was the principal yardstick in the traditional view of effective purchasing. According to this view, the buyer gains two things by playing different suppliers off against one another. One is that competition between suppliers leads them to work more effectively and thus reduce their costs. This has a positive effect on the price for the buying company. The other gain from the previous behaviour was avoidance of over-dependence on a single supplier.

However, our analysis of the strategic importance of purchasing indicates that increased dependence on suppliers is desirable from the points of view both of the developmental and rationalization roles. In fact, supplier dependence is necessary, and openness, mutual trust and a long-term relationship are important ingredients in an effective purchasing strategy.

It is clearly not possible to achieve these attributes in a relationship by applying the previously recommended strategy of playing suppliers off against one another. What is needed, instead, is long-lasting, deepened relationships. We identify this as the new model of purchasing, and it stands in sharp contrast to the traditional one.

It is our ambition to give a picture of what we mean by professional purchasing work under prevailing conditions. This view comprises the theoretical principles on which those conditions are based, their foundations in various contexts, the work done by the individuals responsible for operations, and the organization of purchasing activities. A number of research

projects and our experience from numerous consultancy assign-
ments provide us with the material for this book. It is thus our
aspiration to reflect the research developments from the twenty-
year period in which we have been working with these issues. We
also hasten to add that purchasing is such an extensive, multifaceted field that we cannot possibly cover all its aspects or do
justice to every project which has been carried out. Our selection
is, by necessity, a personal one.

This book does not provide a selection of prescriptions to cure
specific purchasing ailments. Instead, we emphasize the content of
the purchasing function and an awareness of how purchasing
actually works. We have chosen this orientation partly for personal
reasons but also because, in principle, we see purchasing as such a
complex, situation-specific function that there are no simple or
general solutions (other than of the 'Look before you leap!' type).
Every company must formulate its own solution on the basis of its
own specific conditions. For most companies, purchasing is such
a central part of operations that the unique feature of purchasing
is an important aspect of that company's profile.

Our personal motivations are associated with our professional
research roles. Being researchers, we derive greater satisfaction
from studying, structuring and analysing problems than from
formulating specific solutions. Naturally, this does not mean that
we find solutions uninteresting or unimportant for each individual
firm, only that such solutions can seldom be applied directly by
any other company. It is, however, perfectly possible to directly
apply the analytical work which must be done in order to find a
solution.

The book contains nine chapters. In Chapter 2 we describe
the attributes of company purchasing, and the variation in the
purchasing work, depending on what is bought. We go on to
address the issue of which internal factors in the purchasing
firm affect purchasing. Chapter 3 provides examples of changes
observed in company purchasing strategies: one significant finding
is that measures implemented to obtain improvements often have
not had the intended effect. We conclude that this can be
attributed to the fact that the purchasing firm has seen the
problem primarily from its own perspective. In order to succeed
in achieving change, it is important to take the supplier's perspective into account as well. For this reason, Chapter 4 goes on to
analyse the relationship between a purchasing firm and one

supplier. Chapter 5 deals with the relationship to an entire network of customers, suppliers and competitors. In Chapter 6 we report on examples of efforts made by purchasing companies to develop relationships with suppliers, and to develop supplier networks.

Thus Chapters 3 to 6 indicate that purchasing activities are strongly related to other types of activities in an industrial production system, and that many actors (companies and/or individuals) are involved. In light of all this, issues touching on the organization of purchasing operations and activities become vital ones, as do questions of communication between the various actors. Consequently, Chapter 7 deals with organization of purchasing and Chapter 8 with communication aspects related to purchasing.

In the final chapter of the book we analyse the new view of purchasing which permeates our entire argument. This view is a result of a new way of valuing effectiveness in purchasing work. The views of effectiveness espoused by the traditional model and the new one are presented. They are analysed in light of the conditions on which they are based and their consequences. In conclusion we discuss problems and potential associated with changing existing purchasing activities in the direction of the ideas presented in this book.

Chapter 2

Characteristics of purchasing

Purchasing comprises a company's behaviour in relation to its suppliers. The main aim of this chapter is to illustrate and analyse different kinds of behaviour and its potential effects. Before we go on to address these issues, we need to review the characteristics of company purchasing.

This chapter begins with a discussion of the substantial variation in purchasing work, arising from differences in what is being purchased. There are clearly significant differences depending on whether major equipment for a big project or industrial goods for daily use are going to be purchased. We describe and characterize this variation by exemplifying certain specific types of purchases. They are not comprehensive, but do give a good picture of existing differences. The five types used concern purchases of:

- major equipment
- components
- raw materials and processed materials
- MRO supplies (maintenance, repair and operating supplies)
- services.

There are many other factors, in addition to what is being acquired, which affect a company's purchasing. We go on to discuss what internal conditions in a company affect purchasing. Purchasing work goes on in interplay with a number of other company activities. Purchasing of investment goods is an aspect of the company's development activities, as well as being crucial to its production process. Purchasing of raw materials, processed materials and components is closely associated with production and materials handling. In other words, purchasing work is strongly related to the overall running of the company and to how other functions operate. Three sections of this chapter deal with the influence of three specific internal relationships in detail. These are:

- the technological structure of the company
- the organizational structure of the company
- the knowledge and attitude of the personnel with regard to purchasing.

All these factors affect the internal workings of the purchasing company. But one of the most essential tasks of purchasing is to couple a company to given suppliers. This chapter is therefore concluded with a discussion of the main external factor – suppliers and their actions.

PRODUCT-RELATED VARIATIONS IN PURCHASING WORK

Variations in purchasing work related to type of product are an important aspect of purchasing. All companies buy many types of products, but the distribution of their procurement varies. Some companies primarily purchase components, while others buy large volumes of raw materials. In this section we primarily analyse each type of product on its own, while combinations of different products are dealt with under 'Technology'.

Major equipment

The main factor in equipment or systems purchasing is that the products are going to be used for a long period of time. Sometimes the concept of 'lifetime cost' is used to indicate that the costs which arise during use are far greater than the purchase sum which is also, however, often a large amount of money. Consequently, negotiations which precede a purchase are both extensive and complex, and include discussion of the design and functioning of the product in question, and how it is connected or related to the existing machinery and equipment which comes before and after it in the chain of production. Other issues are service, training and spare parts, and another important factor is how the equipment can be successively developed and renewed in the future. Purchasing work is often carried out in project form, as a number of functions are necessarily involved. If there are specialized purchasers, they often play a marginal role to begin with, and this may later develop into a problem, as the technicians may have become locked into unnecessary commercial decisions from an early stage. For the purchasing company, the lifetime costs of the equipment should be central. Attempts have been made to formulate a business transaction including a guaranteed maintenance price. The problem is that it is difficult to establish whether all the conditions are being fulfilled as time goes by. In purchasing major facilities and total projects, the buyer enters into an extensive undertaking. Sometimes a contract may be formulated so that the vendor guarantees some kind of production volume.

One of the main characteristics of this type of purchase is that the choice of equipment may limit the freedom of the buyer for a long time in the future. The purchase of the equipment will largely determine what raw materials and maintenance products will be bought as well. In this way, the acquisition of equipment locks the buyer into a given system, and future development is highly determined by how the technical equipment is developed. In other words, the buyer becomes highly dependent on the ambitions and competence of the supplier. Future possibilities for renovation or upgrading may, for this reason, be important in determining what supplier to choose and what equipment to buy.

Components

Components are identifiable parts of the end product the purchasing company manufactures. They are also often considered important parts by the buyer's customer. In some situations, buyers' customers may even have preferences of their own in relation to the choice of component suppliers. Some components, such as the engine of a lawn-mower, may be particularly significant to the function of the end product, while others may be entirely marginal. From a purchasing point of view, components may be subdivided, in relation to these dimensions, into technical components and adaptation components. (For a similar division see Jansson 1982). Technical components are often manufactured by large companies, working globally. The major buyers of these components have come to be so important that they have a name of their own – OEM companies (original equipment manufacturers). Adaptation components, on the other hand, are products which are not very sophisticated from a technical point of view, but which require some kind of adaptation to the buyer's product. Typical examples of such products include processed and plastic components.

In buying technical components, the function of the component is often important both in itself and in relation to other functions of the end product. For adaptation components, function in relation to the end product is primary. In both cases large volumes are often handled, which means that the storage, handling and administrative costs may be significant. This explains why JIT delivery was initially developed for components.

In relation to a supplier, it is a matter of developing a relationship in which the various problems arising in regard to product specification, means of delivery, etc., can be solved. These are often recurring deliveries, and the point is to take advantage of this repetitive feature to create efficiency. For the purchasing company, it is important for both production, development and marketing personnel to be part of the purchasing work. This is particularly true for technical components. Adaptation components primarily require involvement from the production and materials handling personnel after the design work has been concluded.

Raw materials and processed material

Products which are bought and further processed in-house are referred to as input goods, and include raw materials and material in different stages of processing. From a purchasing point of view, these are often both physically and economically important items. Many of these products have an international market, and their prices fluctuate in relation to the cycles of supply and demand. Consequently, the time dimension takes on a central position when the contract is formulated. When price increases are expected, the purchaser tries to obtain prices that will be stable over as long a period of time as possible, whereas, if prices are falling, the purchaser will avoid committing himself about the price. The strategy of the supplier is basically the opposite.

Another important factor is large volume, which makes handling issues central. When materials are used, there are often leftovers (different types of scrap). How these scrap materials are to be dealt with often becomes an issue of negotiation between buyer and seller. Adaptation of the material often leads to significant rationalization improvements in the buyer's production apparatus.

As this is also often a matter of large volumes of material, such effectiveness improvements may have a major impact on production costs. Another related factor is the relationship between different steps in the refinement process from a technical point of view. There are important connections between how the supplier has dealt with the material and the potential of the buyers to affect their own production process.

It is important that the production personnel and the employees managing materials handling participate with the purchaser when materials and raw materials are to be purchased. Economic competence may also be important, for example, in assessment of currency problems.

MRO supplies

Maintenance, repair and operation supplies are a product group with many articles including fastenings, hand tools, glue and sealants, small grinding equipment, etc. The large number of articles means administrative complexity. As such items are frequently purchased, there are handling consequences. It may also be difficult to plan purchases, as demand is irregular. It may be inconvenient for the purchasing company to run out of such items. The major objective in this type of purchasing is to find effective routines for dealing with the purchasing, rather than optimizing each individual decision. One important aspect deals with the need to increase availability. This may be achieved through standardization and through limiting the product range. Another option is to make order and delivery routines more efficient. In other words, it is more a matter of developing systems to handle purchasing than carrying out each purchase in a certain way. As each product or purchase, in itself, is relatively marginal in terms of volume, many companies have neglected to develop their procurement of this product group, with the consequence that large numbers of small, fragmented purchases become an unnecessary administrative burden.

Services

Services are highly heterogeneous which, of course, affects procurement activities. Areas in which major purchasing developments have been made by large companies include travel, transport, insurance, consulting, and advertising services. In addition, there are a number of simpler services which are similar to product purchasing. These include cleaning and some secretarial and office services. One problem in purchasing services is that the value of the service can only be determined retrospectively. This makes it natural to work with one specific service producer for a long period of time, particularly as there is an important learning effect to be gained.

Construction firms are highly dependent on purchased services. Procurement from service subcontractors accounts for two-thirds of purchasing, and these services are often critical to the completion of the construction job. One problem is that, owing to the uncertainty of the market, it is difficult to co-ordinate this work and to ascertain its quality.

Product-based variations in purchasing

The description of purchasing problems in relation to different types of products shows a substantial variation. There are differences for technical reasons, administrative reasons, and supplier market-related reasons. This variation is very typical for purchasing in all companies and its major effect is that it will always be difficult to find one solution with regard to organization or one administrative routine covering all purchases. We return to this variation from time to time, but it is also important to remember it when we discuss the more general types of purchasing problems.

COMPANY TECHNOLOGY AND ITS EFFECTS ON PURCHASING

In relation to the purchasing company's production, purchasing can be seen as a link to the production facilities of the supplier. This link must be designed in different ways, depending on the company's own technology. If the technology is characterized by low flexibility, purchasing must give priority to security both of technical functions and demands for exact delivery times. If the buying company is characterized by development of unique solutions (products or systems), what will be needed instead are flexibility and adaptability both in purchasing and from the suppliers. In other words, the purchasing method used is directly affected in various ways by the company's technology. Ultimately, the technology will be decisive in terms of priorities about adaptation and flexibility. We will illustrate these effects with a discussion of the purchasing situation for three different types of technology: unit, mass and process manufacturing. Unit manufacturing is the type of technology which gives the producing company most scope in formulation of working operations. In mass production, flexibility is more limited, and there are greater demands for uniformity. The producing (purchasing) company has least freedom of choice in process manufacturing. When the buyer is a unit-manufacturing company, such as a shipyard, it often has extensive contacts with its main suppliers, in which a large number of company functions are involved. In mass-production companies, such as the automotive industry or the appliances industry, the purchasing department may play a significant part in supplier relationships, whereas in process-manufacturing companies such as the chemicals industry, corporate managements handle most of the essential suppliers. Let us now examine the details of how and why there is this variation, and briefly examine the different typical characteristics of the supplier markets.

Purchasing in unit-manufacturing firms

Unit manufacturing is always controlled by a customer order, meaning that each individual product is produced and adapted in response to the demands of a specific customer. Such products may be major pieces of equipment, specially designed components, or entire systems or plants. In a classic study, Woodward (1965) examined the relationships between the various aspects of technology, and their connections with the three functions of development, production and marketing. The sequence found in unit manufacturing firms was marketing – development – production. Although each individual manufacturing sequence was triggered by a sales order, that order was always dependent upon the ability of the development division to design a customer-adapted product. Thus development was the most important function for unit-manufacturing firms. The three functions worked in close interplay, with something of a sequence being identifiable. Technical difficulties and other problems had to be solved continually, in consultation with the customer. As mentioned above, this leads to a demand for extensive contact networks in firms with many functions (Figure 2.1).

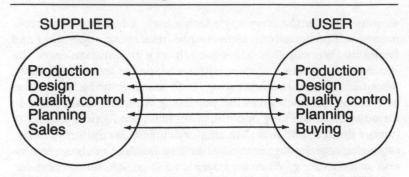

Figure 2.1   Characteristics of supplier relations in unit-production firms (Johanson 1982: 320)

Suppliers to unit-production firms may take on various roles. Suppliers of material and production equipment may play vital ones in relation to their customers. A shipyard, for example, needs large amounts of ship plating, and a transformer producer requires vast quantities of copper wire. However, suppliers of components are often the most important ones. This is because, as a rule, a unit-production firm only has the competence and the production equipment to manufacture certain central components and carry out final assembly. Suppliers of certain components, such as electronic components or bearings, thus become central supplementary resources.

The purchasing company needs access to two different types of external expertise. First, it requires suppliers with resources and expertise to develop, design and produce the technology-intensive components which are part of the end product. A unit-production firm needs to have access to expertise during the development, design, and production phases. It may be beneficial to the buying firm to activate its suppliers of advanced components, as its own customers are often interested in how the various key components work, even when they want to purchase a complete package system. In other words, a component supplier may be more than a supportive resource, and will be more of an active centre-stage actor. During design and production phases, co-ordination among the main component suppliers and between them and the unit-production firm is vital to the completion and finances of the project. The same kind of reciprocal adaptation described above as necessary among internal company functions is also important in relation to these suppliers.

The second type of component suppliers is needed to design and produce a number of components which, although they are simpler ones, may be far from unimportant to the end product. What the buyer requires here is, primarily, an external production resource capable of adapting the product to individual specifications. This requires a clearly more limited kind of expertise than in the first type, and is also easier to specify.

That briefly summarises the demands made on supplier relationships in firms using unit-production technology. This technology also affects the organization of purchasing. Individual projects may be of a magnitude to necessitate setting up a project organization. Most operational purchasing is then carried out by the project group, while responsibility for long-term purchasing work often rests with a central purchasing unit. The link between the short- and long-term purchasing operations then becomes an important one, and may give rise to problems and conflicts between the organizational units. The managers responsible for the technical (functional) content of the product technology thus come to play a dominant part in purchasing work. Therefore, technical dimensions come to weigh heavily throughout. In some cases, particularly in relation to customers with limited financial resources, financing may be an important issue.

Another typical purchasing problem is that the individual customer may have specific desires in relation to component suppliers. This may be because the customer has bought similar units in the past and wishes to maintain some technical or service co-ordination for key components. A large number of functional demands may also give rise to a situation in which only certain suppliers are conceivable. Moreover, several different units may also be involved on the purchasing side. There may be one user, one or more consultancy firms helping with procurement, as well as a contractor who may, for example, bear responsibility for the total project in relation to the user.

Supplier markets for unit-production firms have certain typical characteristics. There are, as a rule, few producers of advanced components, and these are large international companies. There are two fundamental purchasing strategies for a buying company. One – perhaps the most common – is to seek close co-operation with one supplier and only have sporadic contact with the others. The alternative strategy is to strive to allocate its purchasing among several suppliers in an attempt to avoid association with one supplier only. The disadvantage of this second strategy is that the purchaser cannot make use of the suppliers' potential support in marketing and development, as is possible with the first strategy. On the other hand, the second strategy makes it easier to adapt to the preferences of the customer with regard to the choice of supplier.

There are often many conceivable suppliers for simpler components, and distance becomes a factor. Geographical proximity leads to decreased transport costs and facilitates regular contact, which is important in terms of coping with the necessary adaptations.

In summary, purchasing operations in unit-production firms are characterized by solving problems as they arise. Suppliers are important from the points of view of expertise and development, as it is impossible for these firms to have access to the extensive necessary expertise themselves. Moreover, suppliers may be important co-actors in marketing work, which is generally characterized by a large number of parties being involved on the purchasing side.

Purchasing in mass-production firms

From a technological point of view, the main characteristic of series or mass-production firms is their rigidity. In order to attain a high degree of production efficiency, which is absolutely decisive to the competitiveness of the company, precision and exactness in planning and production are important. To achieve this, stable and secure material and component flows are necessary. The importance of these flows can also be described by indicating that efficient handling of them may lead to great savings potential. It is no coincidence that the concept of JIT was developed and has mainly been applied at firms using this technology. In other words, stability is one of the main purchasing strategy objectives of mass-production firms. Yet they also need change. If a firm is to keep up with the competition, it will need to develop its materials and components, and will therefore have to carry out development work in co-operation with its materials and component suppliers. Thus there are concomitant demands for stability and change. For this reason, a purchasing company has to balance the need for stability in day-to-day operations against the need of change for development. This is true both of individual relationships and in the firm's total network of material- and component-supplier relationships.

Purchasing of equipment poses slightly different problems. Production of equipment is vital to a mass-production firm, as it determines the cost status of the firm. Furthermore, production is so integrated that all equipment must be reciprocally adapted. Generally, the firm tries to solve this problem by maintaining close co-operation with its main equipment suppliers.

Mass-production firms were early to professionalize their purchasing functions. This occurred because component purchasing was both so important from a financial point of view and so obviously problematic that it required specialist handling. Central purchasing departments grew up, and rapidly became internal power factors. The need for planning and stability paved the way for this centralization. Consequently, purchasing departments have come to play a central role in supplier relationships – not only formally but also in reality (see Figure 2.2). This is particularly true for regular contacts. At the selling company, however, more people and functions are involved. When major changes occur, such as the introduction of a new model, the technicians at the purchasing company play an important role, and are in direct contact with the technicians at the selling firm.

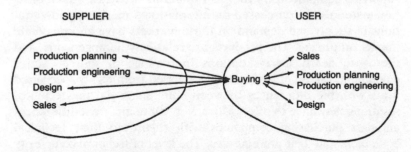

Figure 2.2 Characteristics of supplier relations in mass-production firms (Johanson 1982: 321)

One common characteristic of mass-production firms is that they are aggressive buyers who demand adaptation from their suppliers. This is particularly true when, as is often the case, the suppliers are small companies. And the buyers are far less eager to make any kind of adaptations themselves.

The supplier markets from which mass-production firms buy

may be roughly divided into two categories. They purchase their more advanced components and materials on markets which may be described as international oligopolies, with a small number of large, highly specialized producers. These markets are similar to those described in the section on unit-production firms, and are dealt with using similar strategies. The other category is more one of local markets with smaller subcontractors who produce a number of simpler components and/or materials. These are what have, for example, long been referred to in the automotive industry as the 'subcontractor network'.

In summary, purchasing work in mass-production firms is characterized by the organization of cost-beneficial supplier relationships with component- and material-producing firms. There are also examples in this type of firm of buyers active several links back in the chain, who build up their supplier networks in a highly systematic fashion.

Purchasing in process-producing firms

From the point of view of purchasing, a process-producing firm is characterized by its total dependence on a supply of raw materials for its everyday activities. In the same way, it is dependent on a supply of equipment in order to expand its activities. Much of its raw materials are purchased on international markets, and variations in supply and demand on these markets have an immediate impact on pricing. The products are relatively homogeneous, and there are nearly always options for change of source. Major equipment, on the other hand, is purchased from highly specialized firms with big differences between companies and the technical solutions they have to offer. Moreover, there are great differences amongst purchasing companies with regard to their technical equipment and their prerequisites. The level of technical complexity is thus increased with regard to the purchasing of new equipment. This means that two extreme cases characterize purchasing in a process-producing firm. When their needs are completely standardized they can be satisfied by buying from a raw-materials exchange market. When the needs are completely unique, they can only be satisfied by buying from a highly specialized supplier. Most process-producing firms have both these kinds of purchasing.

The supply problems in the purchasing of raw materials are often of a logistics nature, as long as demand does not exceed production capacity. However, when shortage situations arise, supply becomes critical. Some firms choose backward integration, meaning that they acquire their supplier or source of raw materials in order to ensure the supply. For example, paper industries often own forests, just as in the past steel mills often owned mines. Alongside its benefits, one disadvantage of ownership is, of course, limited freedom. In terms of acquisitions, process-producing companies always need to balance security and control against the potential for rapid adaptation in situations of price fluctuations, currency changes, or political upheaval. A company which chooses not to integrate backward can also increase its security by entering into agreements with regard to fixed deliveries over long periods of time. Such fixed contracts are often used, for example, to cover two-thirds of a given type of demand, while the rest is bought on the open market when it is most advantageous from a short-term perspective. There is certainly a speculative element in this. It is tempting to try to tie down a price when demand is expected to rise, and to do the opposite when demand is expected to fall. Some companies try to take advantage of this type of variation, while others insure themselves against it. There are generally very small differences among suppliers of raw materials. In some cases, though, apparently small technical differences may be very important to the purchasing company. Such differences may make themselves known in production disturbances when a new supplier is used, and may also be important factors to consider when deciding on investments.

Equipment purchases are almost always technically complex, and are therefore generally conducted by a project group. Major investments require extensive preparatory work, in which suppliers must also be involved. It is difficult to keep up relation-ships with suppliers over time, since major investments are made at irregular intervals. Certain replacement and spare parts are bought on a regular basis, but these purchases are normally handled by personnel who are not involved in purchasing the major equipment. Such contacts can be maintained to some extent at conferences and trade fairs, and both suppliers and customers take every advantage of such opportunities, but these contacts are often too superficial to satisfy the actual need for exchange of information. Some firms try to solve this problem by developing close collaboration with one supplier – sometimes they even enter into an ownership association – in order to be able to work actively for the successive improvements of the plant which are always needed. This type of collaboration makes it easier to establish the necessary initial contacts for large projects, but may unfortunately also lead to situations in which suppliers feel over-confident, and cease to do their very best.

From an organizational point of view, this highly fragmented picture of purchasing leads to important roles being played by people at the firms who are not supposed to work with purchasing. With regard to equipment purchasing, the heaviest involvement is that of the project manager and his co-opted specialists, all of whom are normally technicians of different kinds. There are often purchasing specialists for raw materials, but they generally work extremely closely with corporate management. Raw-materials purchasing is so financially important that, as a rule, management wishes to have some direct influence. Other product purchasing is generally carried out by purchasers who may, in some cases, be associated with purely storage-oriented tasks. On the whole, the corporate management will have more influence over purchases in firms using process-production technologies than in unit- or mass-production firms (see Figure 2.3).

THE EFFECTS OF ORGANIZATIONAL STRUCTURE ON PURCHASING

Our discussion of the effects of different types of technology on purchasing has also indicated the importance of organizational structure. Different types of purchasing situations place different demands on this structure. Let us now look more closely at the

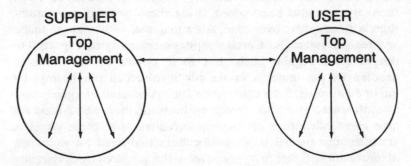

Figure 2.3 Characteristics of supplier relations in process-producing firms (Johanson 1982: 323)

effects of organizational structure on purchasing. We begin with two examples of how purchasing may be organized.

Mr Andersson, purchasing manager, is in his office, at company headquarters in Stockholm. He has just concluded a conversation with a supplier in Gothenburg in which he has lodged a serious complaint. The supplier was late with a delivery, failed to notify the company, and the result was production disturbances at the Karlstad plant. Yesterday, Andersson was roundly lectured by the plant manager, and now he has passed the message along. He is very familiar with the supplying firm, and turned to someone high up in the corporate hierarchy to emphasize his statement that, if this happens one more time, his company intends to change suppliers. He is certain that he has made himself understood, and now hopes that he will never hear from Karlstad again regarding this supplier.

Mr Pettersson, purchasing manager of a completely different company, has just rung off after a similar telephone conversation. Pettersson's office is in Örebro, in the same building as the production unit whose purchases he manages. That unit is part of a larger company with a central purchasing co-ordinator, but he has no operational responsibility. Pettersson is having problems with a supplier in Sundsvall who has trouble keeping his deadlines, mainly because he gets contradictory messages from different units within the purchasing company. Several units are using the same product and, owing to a shortage in recent months, tough competition has evolved regarding volumes. Pettersson and the supplier agree by phone to try to develop a routine together with the other units within the buying company in order to solve the problem.

As this example shows, purchasing is affected by the organizational structure a company chooses. There is no doubt that a central purchasing unit makes it easier to specialize in relation to different supplier markets. On the other hand, a central purchasing unit makes it more difficult to keep in touch with the divisions using the products. In a highly decentralized firm, it is easy to keep up internal contacts within each of the local units and also to stay in close contact with suppliers used frequently. It is more difficult to co-ordinate between the different units belonging to the same firm and to have a clear external overview. In the next section we discuss the significance of organizational structure, with these two examples in mind. We begin by describing and analysing a typical centralized purchasing function, and then compare it with its decentralized equivalent.

Centralized purchasing

Centralization of purchasing makes it possible to gather the resources to be used, and carry out activities from one place. There are two main advantages of this structure. The first is co-ordination among different parts of the firm in relation to individual suppliers. The second is that it becomes possible to allocate resources, primarily manpower resources, more effectively. When all resources are in one place, they become manageable. The main disadvantage is one of internal communication. A sense of us versus them between production and purchasing can easily arise, and purchasing becomes a specialization rather than an integral part of operations. However, making purchasing a specialization also gives it some status, and when a centralized purchasing unit works well, there is no doubt that it has a powerful position in the firm. This is also true in relation to various suppliers. It is easy for a centralized purchasing department to gain a good overview of the market and to discuss the total situation with each supplier regularly. With a larger purchasing volume than of individual units, the purchasing department also gains a stronger negotiating position.

In a centralized purchasing department, work is generally divided according to product type. In other words, different groups of purchasers are responsible for different product groups. There might be a raw-materials group, a components group, a group responsible for investment products, and one for general materials. Within each group there may then be sub-allocation so that one purchaser takes responsibility for one or more specific products. In this way the purchaser can become a specialist in one area with regard to both products and suppliers. Table 2.1 shows typical contact profiles for purchasers responsible for purchasing different products. The characteristic feature, particularly for the raw-materials purchaser, is that a large proportion of their time is allocated to contacts with suppliers. Because purchasing is centralized and often separate from the production unit, another feature is that planning meetings are the most common type of contact, and the everyday work life of these purchasers is filled with planning meetings. Another important observation is that

Table 2.1 Contact profiles for four purchasers specializing in buying different products

| | Purchaser of raw material | Purchasers of two different components | | Purchaser of equipment |
		A	B	
Internal contacts with users	9	17	21	42
Contacts with suppliers	56	22	22	13
Contacts within the purchasing department	16	12	10	9
Purchasing activities which do not involve contacts	19	49	47	36
	100	100	100	100

Source: Håkansson and Wootz 1975: 65

purchasers spend a large proportion of their total time on contacts. Managing purchasing is, to a large extent, a matter of communication, keeping in touch both internally and with suppliers.

Decentralized purchasing activities

Fundamentally, a decentralized organizational model means that purchasing is not a specialist function, but rather an integral part of a larger context, which means purchasing cannot be dealt with separately. It must, therefore, be closely associated with the total operations of the company or unit of which it is a part. Often there are one or more specially appointed individuals (purchasers) responsible for activities. These individuals may have other responsibilities as well. At the same time, the other line personnel are highly involved. For example, at a construction site, the general manager and supervisor plus the foremen are always very much involved, at least in the selection of major subcontractors and materials suppliers. This results in natural co-ordination of internal operations, which is usually a good thing, but it is also generally difficult to establish good co-ordination with other units in the firm. It facilitates co-operation with local suppliers, but the increased distance leads to worsening of the contact interface with national suppliers, in relation to whom big construction companies tend to function as if they were composed of a large number of small construction companies. Activities become fragmented, and at times competition arises among divisions of the same firm. In shortage situations, there are many examples, both from stationary industries and construction industries, of different divisions in the same firm striving to outbid one another for goods from a particular supplier.

One clear problem in highly decentralized companies is the reduced professionalism of the purchaser. He becomes a far greater generalist, needing to have the competence to purchase across an extremely large product range. In order to move in the direction of rectifying this problem, some companies such as SKF have begun working with decentralized specialization. This means that different local units are appointed to represent the whole company in relation to a given product group. At SKF these are referred to as IPCs – international purchasing centres. Each IPC is responsible for internal collection and co-ordination of the requirements of SKF as a whole, on the basis of which the company tries to achieve total solutions with individual suppliers. This kind of specialization means that more funds are allocated to monitoring, following and influencing the company's main supplier markets. These centres also make it increasingly possible to take advantage of the clout of the entire company in purchasing, thus benefiting from one of the positive traits of centralized operations.

Organizational effects in summary

The principle of organization chosen by a firm for purchasing has a major impact on how its work is done. The actions of individuals depend both on how they have been trained and on what opportunities for specialization they are given, as well as on the characteristics of their environments. A purchaser working with other purchasers will be influenced by different values and attitudes than a purchaser working with planners and technicians. Thus, although the structure of an organization affects working methods, it is also a result of both how the company functions from a technical point of view and in accordance with what principles it is structured. If the company as a whole is decentralized, it is impossible to have a centralized purchasing department. If the company's technology is fragmented, it is far more difficult to have a central purchasing department than if the company as a whole is structured around a well-defined technology. Organizationally, then, there are many factors posing restrictions, but there have still been relatively great general changes in the structure of purchasing organizations in the 1980s. The evident trend has been towards decentralization. The changes in how purchasing is seen, briefly mentioned in Chapter 1, have been an important driving force, as has the general corporate decentralization in profit centres.

PERSONNEL KNOWLEDGE OF AND ATTITUDES TOWARDS PURCHASING

In many firms, purchasing suffers from low status. This is partly attributable to historical factors, as purchasing has developed both from traditional accounting and bookkeeping departments and from the storage operations of companies. Thus it was seen as a function which was supposed to 'keep papers and things in order', as one purchasing manager described it. Purchasing was also an expense for the firm – a 'necessary evil'. There are still very few companies which consider it a merit to have worked in purchasing. Although there are clear exceptions to this gloomy description, it still applies generally to the in-house status of purchasing at most firms. From this point of view, it is also quite obvious that being a purchasing manager has not been regarded as being particularly complicated or requiring a high degree of expertise. 'All they [purchasers] have to do is sit around waiting for the suppliers to undercut one another' is quite a typical comment, although the person who said it did not mean it literally. So purchasing managers have a great deal to work against in many firms when, for instance, they request increased resources for purchasing or for expertise-improving activities.

In Chapter 1, we also found that the attitude towards suppliers was traditionally more one of hostility than co-operation, of being on opposite sides rather than the same one. This implies that suppliers have been seen not as dependable partners who contribute in various ways to the competitiveness of one's company, but as unreliable necessities doing whatever they can to benefit themselves, and who need to have the squeeze put on them whenever possible. This view of the supplier has, of course, further emphasized the negative attitude towards purchasing.

Many companies stress the importance of purchasers having commercial expertise. This was particularly true in the past, but there was never much clarity as to what this actually meant. Language courses are one very common form of further training offered to purchasing employees. Another is courses in law, particularly contractual law, and a third is computer courses. In comparison with the marketing side, in courses held for purchasing departments purchasing itself is seldom analysed and discussed.

The attitudes and qualifications traditionally and still today associated with purchasing may pose the most difficult obstacle to overcome in terms of rapid development of the purchasing function. Some companies have closed their purchasing departments altogether because they have found it impossible to develop the existing organization. Closing down gives a firm space to build up something completely new over time. Other companies have invested heavily in changing their purchasing departments. In later sections we exemplify and analyse this type of change.

SUPPLIER BEHAVIOUR

A buyer is one player in a game which takes at least two to play. The other must be a supplier, who affects the purchaser through his behaviour. When, for example, a purchasing company seeks new types of supplier collaboration, many of the problems which have arisen have been owing to suppliers' difficulties in adapting to this new kind of interaction. They are extremely interested as long as questions remain at the discussion stage, but find it far more difficult to go further to implement real changes in their operations. Analogous with our discussion of the purchasing side, individuals on the supplier side may be locked into situations presenting problems of technology, organization, attitude or expertise. Technically, it may be difficult for a selling firm to adapt to the demands of individual customers, just as it may be difficult to make technical communication penetrate through to the individuals meant to deal with these issues. Technical restrictions on the selling side may, then, obstruct the development of new forms of collaboration.

Similarly, the marketing organization built up by the supplier may pose an obstacle. It is often outward orientated, that is, structured to spread the selling company's own message in an effective way. However, it may be far more poorly equipped to collect and transmit the demands and desires of the purchasing company to people within the selling company when, for example, buyer and seller are trying to collaborate more closely. Perhaps technicians in both production and development need to be involved, and it may not be nearly as clear as it was in the past that the marketing personnel are to be the main actors.

Another related problem is cost awareness and cost accounting. In the more intimate type of collaboration now being developed, both parties must be extremely familiar with their cost structures. In this respect the selling company's picture may be just as incomplete as that of the buying firm – at least with regard to different types of indirect costs. There are a small number of examples of selling firms that have tried to develop their cost accounting, for example, in order to be able to estimate the costs for which different individual customers are accountable. Since revenues (at least in pecuniary terms) can generally be seen or easily made available from the accounts, it is possible to calculate revenues per customer. But only a very small number of companies do this. The vast majority do not have this information, and find it extremely difficult to estimate the distribution. This also means that it is difficult for them to see potential savings in buyer–seller relations.

Just as there are attitude problems on the purchasing side, there are attitude problems on the selling side. Sales personnel often expect themselves, for example, to be the active ones, the ones who make proposals and presentations, and who present arguments, while they expect the purchasers to be relatively passive, waiting for sales initiatives. Pricing and price discussions are also expected to be in focus. Employees with strong preconceptions about this attitude may find it difficult to adjust to a situation where the seller and buyer first sit down and analyse goods, information and cash flows, especially as this may necessitate greater changes in the working methods of the seller than of the buyer.

INFLUENTIAL FACTORS – CONCLUDING COMMENTS

In this chapter we have discussed a number of factors which shape or affect purchasing work in individual firms in various ways. The text has pointed out certain connections between these factors. The technology used by the firm largely determines the product mix to be purchased, which in turn decides which suppliers and supplier markets are of interest. On the whole, this creates a structure which more or less naturally determines the structure of the purchasing organization. The various influencing factors are thus reciprocally dependent, and their interplay gives rise to typical purchasing problem patterns. Yet there is still such great individual variation that it is advantageous to define them one by one despite their interrelations.

Seen as a whole, these factors determine what purchasing questions are relevant and what purchasing problems can be solved. Consequently, changes in technology and organization have an impact on purchasing. For this reason, when a company considers changes in technology and organization, the purchasing consequences should also be analysed. Furthermore, the opposite is also important. That is, in order to make it possible to do the purchasing in a certain way, the organization or the technology may have to be altered. These affecting factors determine the framework for purchasing, although they are neither absolute nor completely inflexible. The limiting factors may perfectly well be broken in various ways, but such attempts must be conscious, and they require perseverance. This is also a generally more resource-intensive choice than working within the existing framework.

Chapter 3

Central purchasing issues: a reassessment

As described in Chapters 1 and 2, the 1980s marked the emergence of a new view of purchasing of which the evolution began earlier, but the tangible effects were first notable during that decade. Generally, this change can be described as a transition from considering purchasing as a matter of getting the lowest possible prices to seeing purchasing as a function responsible for supplying the firm with input resources in an efficient way. One consequence is that the strategic importance of purchasing has increased considerably.

This chapter analyses the impact of this change on these three central purchasing issues:

- The balance between external purchasing and in-house production
- The design of the supplier structure
- The development of relationships with individual suppliers.

The first issue deals with the decision of what to produce in-house and what to purchase externally. This type of analysis (make-or-buy analysis) is firmly rooted in purchasing. It is thus nothing new but has, over time, gained importance owing to specialization of production and development.

The second issue deals with the design of the supplier structure (the number of suppliers and how they are organized in relation to one another). The dominant view of purchasing has led to fragmentation in relation to this issue. The prevailing purchasing philosophy resulted in an increasing number of suppliers, which increased the need for co-ordination. This led to a rapid rise in indirect costs which, when it began to be noted, resulted in a change in purchasing methods. By decreasing its number of suppliers, a firm can reduce its co-ordination costs.

The third issue deals with development of relations to individual suppliers. The main question is what role each supplier can play for the purchasing firm. This can be broken down into sub-issues dealing with how intimate co-operation should be and what it should involve, and thus touches on quality in supplier relations.

None of these three fundamental strategic dimensions is new. They have all been important elements of purchasing work by tradition, although the second and third have been less explicit than the first. What is new, as is demonstrated below, is that the view of these questions has changed so dramatically that we may very well speak of a revolution in purchasing.

Although these three issues, especially the second and third, are also mutually dependent, we deal with them in separate sections. We begin by discussing how each issue is analysed both in the literature and in different companies. We describe the arguments used to promote various lines of development, and illustrate with changes in corporate behaviour over time.

MAKE OR BUY

One of the key issues in supply strategy is the decision of the purchasing company either to produce in-house or to purchase externally. This has been a fundamental problem since the birth of industrial manufacturing, yet not until recently does it seem to have been viewed by firms as an important strategic issue. Culliton (1942) found that many managers claimed that they had no problems when asked about the make-or-buy dilemma. In his opinion, this response should be interpreted as their lacking the ability to acknowledge the existence of this major strategic problem area. More recent literature, too, indicates that there is still an absence of such awareness (see, for example, Janch and Wilson 1979, and Leenders and Nollet 1984).

According to Janch and Wilson, managers have tended to ignore the make-or-buy conflict or, when they have noted it, they have often left decisions in the hands of the purchasing department, whereas assessments have been made more on the basis of retrospective cost data than strategic considerations.

Despite the distinct lack of strategic analysis of this issue, one clear trend can be noted with regard to developments over time. In 1942, Culliton stated that companies had very little to go on when deciding whether to make or buy. He did not even feel that his own dissertation was successful in identifying the pros and cons of different methods in different situations. His experience did make him of the opinion that a 'buy' strategy was generally preferable to a 'make' one.

He reached this conclusion using arguments emphasizing the disadvantages of in-house production (rapid market changes and the major difficulties associated with the transition from make to buy). The advantage of external purchasing he identified, writing in 1942, was positive development of independent suppliers' production technologies and transport systems, so that they would satisfy high demands for supplier performance. In light of subsequent developments in production technology and transport systems, it is hardly surprising that 'buy' has taken the upper hand over 'make'. Another way of seeing the same phenomenon is to express it as a reduction of the degree of vertical integration in the production system. (Vertical integration means that the company covers the entire range of production stages.)

Dirrheimer and Hübner (1983) analysed vertical integration in the automotive industry, and their findings indicate that the degree of integration varies substantially among firms and from one country to another. However, all investigated units showed reductions in vertical integration during the five-year study period. American automobile manufacturers had the highest degree of integration. Hayes and Abernathy (1980) warn against too high a degree of backward vertical integration, because this may limit the prerequisites for and capability of creative thinking and development. For this reason, they prefer a purchase strategy as a means of avoiding becoming locked into obsolete technology.

The degree of vertical integration has also fallen for industry as a whole. Kumpe and Bolwijn (1988) found that numerous production firms have become increasingly dependent on innovative subcontractors, who have proved able to contribute to making both production and development work more effective. The authors also found that purchasing companies have succeeded in retaining sufficient control over their supply situation without having to own their suppliers, by encouraging suppliers to consider themselves 'part of the family' of the purchasing company. In other words, these authors see various types of collaboration and joint efforts as a way of obtaining the benefits of ownership without the corresponding disadvantages. The same observation can be made with regard to the automotive industry, where Gadde and Grant (1984) noted the occurrence of various kinds of 'quasi-integration'. Examples of such intermediate forms include joint investments in production tools, loans and credit guarantees, and ownership of minority shares in one another's companies.

We have found that the degree of vertical integration has decreased over time. This is a result of heightened awareness of the potential of using external resources, and it will be interesting to see whether this trend continues and grows.

Miles and Snow (1986) are of the opinion that this will be the case. They think that changes in the environment and new competition situations will mean that, in the future, industry will be characterized by entirely new organizational forms. This principle is illustrated in Figure 3.1. The main feature is that the functions described in the Figure are performed by separate companies, each specialized in its respective activity.

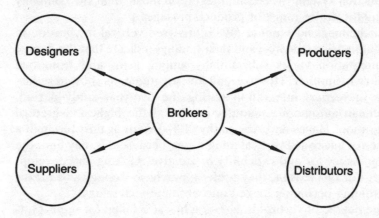

Figure 3.1 A new way of organizing industrial systems (Miles and Snow 1986: 65)

This type of industrial system is held together by brokers, central actors, who take responsibility for the necessary functions, but do not necessarily carry them out themselves. The system functions through these central actors, who organize the various specialist activities. The constellation of actors varies, with interchangeability among the different specialist categories.

Let us return to Kumpe and Bolwijn (1988) to illustrate the uncertainty of the future. Their answer to the question of whether vertical integration is going to go on decreasing is a firm 'no'. In their opinion, it is not even going to remain static. Rather, they now expect the pendulum to swing back in the direction of increasing vertical integration. They explain this as being attributable to one characteristic of most industrial systems today: that profitability distribution is such that the companies in the final stages of the chain of refinement (assembly and distribution) are the ones which make money, while those at the beginning of the flow chain (development and component production) are in great need of investments in order for the competitive power of the whole chain to be maintained. In the short term, end-assembly firms may maximize revenues by decreasing vertical integration, but the long-term effects of this may be catastrophic. A company which chooses this strategy may run its own strategic component suppliers out of business, and then find itself forced to purchase components from a competitor.

Thus Kumpe and Bolwijn claim that, owing to the necessity of economic investment in the first links in the chain of refinement, the circle must be closed with increased vertical integration. Independent component producers subjected to tough price competition will not manage to generate the necessary funds to stay competitive. In the opinion of these authors, then, today's trend towards decreased vertical integration is entirely unrealistic in a long-term perspective.

The contradictory research results presented above may be explained, to some extent, by their concentration on the formal degree of vertical integration. Although this has decreased, it may have been replaced by informal integration – referred to above as quasi-integration (coined by Blois 1971). If that is the case – and there are many indications that it is – then we will not necessarily see the pendulum swing predicted by Kumpe and Bolwijn, but it will also mean that purchasing companies are less free to switch supplier than Miles and Snow and others claim. In any case, we are indisputably moving towards a new kind of industrial organization with many types of corporate product supply. Instead of either 'pure' in-house production or 'pure' purchasing from completely independent suppliers as the dominant form, we may find that intermediate forms are superior.

As described in Chapter 1, today even small and medium-sized companies depend more on purchasing than on in-house production. On an average, remuneration to suppliers accounted for 50 per cent of total costs, but with substantial variation. Important underlying factors, of course, include the type of technology the company uses and its mode of production, but even firms with similarities in these respects exhibit considerable variation. In light of this, it should be reasonable to conclude that for many firms there is still a great deal to be gained in increasing their proportion of purchasing. Others have probably already reached or even surpassed the level which gives the greatest long-term survival capacity.

The discussion above can be summarized in three points.

1 The general trend is for companies to purchase more instead of producing themselves, in other words, to move towards a greater degree of specialization. Firms choose increasingly to use specialized suppliers instead of in-house production. On average, suppliers already account for half of most companies' turnover. Another result of specialization is a change in what is purchased. Today, even design and development are, more and more, being purchased externally.

2 How far this process can go is an open question. Some scholars predict a pendulum movement, such that the future will mean a return to an increased proportion of in-house production. We have some doubt about this hypothesis, and see the current development as a tendency towards successive specialization which will only be broken under very particular circumstances. This may mean that the proportion of purchasing at some point in the future ceases to expand, but at present we are far from that point.

3 One of the phenomena that makes us believe in continued specialization with regard both to production and development is the emergence of intermediate forms, quasi-integration or extended supplier relationships, which grew up in the 1980s. These forms both describe developments to date and probably also indicate a future form towards which companies have only taken the very first steps.

DESIGN OF THE SUPPLIER STRUCTURE

Design of the supplier structure can be divided into two issues. One is the number of suppliers, the other how the suppliers are organized.

In one way, the number of suppliers has never, in itself, been a key issue in purchasing strategy. Firms have avoided becoming over-dependent on individual suppliers. Historically, therefore, effective purchasing has been seen as characterized by having a number of suppliers, with the aim of dealing with the risks. This policy also has positive effects in that suppliers compete with one another. It has undergone radical change, however, and consequences of this change are discussed below.

One reason for the change is that it was found to be highly advantageous to co-operate closely with individual suppliers. For this reason, many firms have begun to work actively towards changing their entire supplier structures, which has given the issue strategic significance for the first time. In the past it was not uncommon for management not even to know how many suppliers the firms used or who they were. The supplier structure as a whole was considered irrelevant. Because the main aim was to make every individual purchase as cheap as possible, the structure as such was uninteresting.

Number of suppliers

The choice between single sourcing (one supplier per product) and multiple sourcing (several suppliers per product) is a classic problem in purchasing strategy. As we have seen, the traditional view of efficient purchasing led to the use of multiple sourcing, since competition among suppliers was given high priority. Melin (1986) points out that using many suppliers leads to better price-level control, and to increased supply security for the buyer. Puto et al. (1985) show that multiple sourcing is an important strategy used by purchasing companies to reduce their purchasing uncertainty.

We have seen that multiple sourcing as a purchasing strategy was on the rapid decline in the 1980s. Newman (1988) found that there was a distinct trend towards single sourcing, or at least in the direction of a substantial reduction of the number of suppliers. This has been most visible in the automotive industry. For example, Raia (1988) showed that Chrysler reduced its number of cable-sleeve suppliers from fourteen to three, and of paint from five to two (one for the US plants and one for the Canadian ones). In a major study of 1,024 suppliers between 1983 and 1988, Helper (1989) found that the average number of competitors any supplier has for his product in relation to any given customer had fallen from 2.0 to 1.5, while the average contract period had nearly doubled (from 1.3 to 2.5 years). This type of development at component level naturally has substantial effects on the total number of suppliers. Thus, between 1984 and 1988, the Volvo Car Company reduced its number of suppliers from 850 to 614, and the SAAB passenger-car division was working to decrease its supplier stock from 500 to 300 (*Dagens Industri* 1988). Between 1981 and 1987 Ford USA reduced its number of suppliers from 3,200 to 2,100 (Burt 1989).

This development was not limited to the automotive industry. Morgan (1987) reported that Rank Xerox, which had over 5,000 suppliers in 1981, had just over 300 five years later. In a British study, four out of five firms reported a continued reduction of their supplier bases. They intended to decrease the number of suppliers by up to 50 per cent over a period of three to five years (Galt and Dale 1991).

This trend stands in marked contrast to what has traditionally been considered effective purchasing. Newman (1988) states that just one decade ago this clear trend toward single sourcing would have been considered an 'invitation to disaster', as it means losing the benefits of risk spreading and price control which come from having many suppliers. It is the new view of purchasing which explains this shift in strategy. Today, one might say that single sourcing does, in fact, result in increased security of supply, as more effective materials-supply systems can be established in a firm that uses fewer suppliers. With regard to price control and costs, Newman (1988) was of the opinion that the price competition considered to be the result of multiple sourcing is often illusory, as it is not possible to distinguish the separate costs in the total price. Håkansson and Wootz (1984) described the same problem as follows: when indirect costs related to purchasing are higher than direct ones (primarily price), or when they are more open to influence, extensive co-operation with one supplier leads to lower costs than would have been the case if many suppliers had the chance to compete. This principle is illustrated in Figure 3.2, taken from an article which clearly indicates the advantages this kind of purchasing concentration brought to one construction company (Asplund and Wootz 1986).

In an American study, Hay (1988) found that purchasers consider it possible to accomplish many things in relation to one or two suppliers of a component which would be impossible if

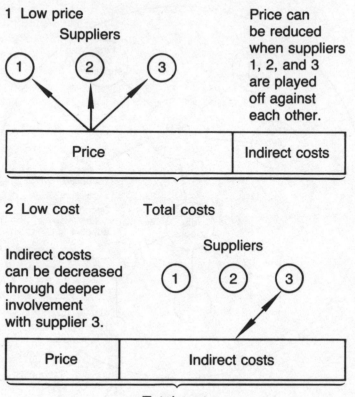

Figure 3.2 Two strategic principles for purchasing (Asplund and Wootz, 1986: 61)

more suppliers were used. On the other hand, this new situation is understandably frustrating to a purchaser who is accustomed to behaving in an entirely different way.

Organization of the supplier structure

The other dimension in the design of the supplier structure is related to its organization. For an illustration of the effects of different organizational forms, we refer to a study by Gadde and Grant (1984). They report that in a certain product area, General Motors (GM) had 3,500 suppliers, Volvo 800 and Toyota 168. The difference between Volvo and GM was mainly attributable to

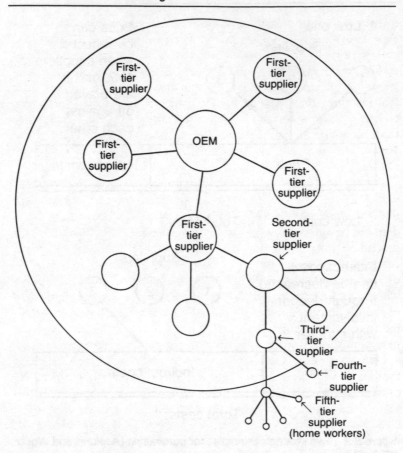

Figure 3.3 Japanese supplier hierarchy (Blenkhorn and Noori, 1990: 23)

differences in total production and number of plants. This makes the Toyota figures difficult to understand. Although Toyota is far larger than Volvo (more in the class of GM), it has a substantially smaller number of firms supplying directly. This is not because it takes fewer components to construct a Toyota, but because the two companies organize their supplier structures very differently.

Toyota, like many other Japanese companies, has built up a hierarchical supplier structure, in which firms in the first tier have been given responsibility for product development, systems undertakings and JIT deliveries (see Figure 3.3). These suppliers are each highly specialized in production and development in their own component areas. Second-tier firms are smaller, have less expertise, generally specialize in a narrower range of products, and work with production and/or processing (for instance, galvanization and thermal treatment). Third-tier suppliers are correspondingly less sophisticated in terms of competence and activities (for instance, they may produce plastic parts). At the fourth-tier, which sometimes occurs, we find small enterprises, and sometimes there is a fifth tier with work done in the home. Details of the Japanese system and its characteristics may be found in Nishiguchi (1987).

During the 1980s, automobile manufacturers in the Western world actively tried to change their supplier structures to be more like the Japanese models. This has, however, proved to be a demanding process. One of the reasons is the hesitation an individual purchaser may feel in the fact of such an extensive reappraisal of an established strategy. Another is that it may be difficult to find suppliers with the desired characteristics. Suppliers who succeed in remaining at the forefront of developments are probably not the typical initial subcontractors. Lamming (1989) has found that GM in the US have had trouble implementing their new philosophy, owing to a shortage of system suppliers.

One important comment in conjunction with this issue is that there are connections between the various roles played by purchasing described in Chapter 1. The activities discussed in this section fall under the rationalization and developmental roles. Closer co-operation with a smaller number of suppliers may make it possible to get more out of the remaining ones, thanks to more efficient materials flows, lower indirect costs and more effective development work. It is also clear that these measures will have significant effects on structures. One reasonable consequence of changes in purchasing behaviour is that the status of technically competent suppliers with good resources will be reinforced, while many other suppliers with a shortage of resources will vanish from the market.

For many purchasing firms, this will mean that geographical distance to the remaining suppliers increases. This is a problem, because physical distance is important both in terms of supply security and communication on complex issues. The dilemma is a familiar one to the Swedish automotive industry, which has traditionally depended on local suppliers, but is now predicting increased exchange with international suppliers. The same problem complex applies on even larger markets. In the opinion of Cayer (1988), the American manufacturing industry has increased its purchasing activities in other countries (low-price producers or producers of special qualities), with the result that today, for numerous components, there are no domestic producers at all. This is considered a major problem, not only for individual buyers but from a national perspective as well. If crucial sub-contractors are lost, the next step may be the disappearance of the manufacturing industry.

THE QUALITY OF SUPPLIER RELATIONS

The main reason for reducing the number of suppliers has been to give the firm better potential for working closely with the remaining ones. Two effects have been in focus: the reduction of a number of costs, i.e. increased effectiveness on the basis of a relationship; and development, i.e. exploiting supplier relations to improve the firm's own technical development. As technical progress can also mean increased effectiveness, there are many cases of overlap here as well, but the important thing is that the content of relationships is affected, and consequently also how relationships are to be assessed. Let us examine these two effects in detail.

Increased effectiveness through supplier relations

Rationalization work covers a number of day-to-day operations to improve price and delivery terms and make co-operation and administrative work more efficient. One good example is a company which introduced system contracts with one of its main suppliers, primarily to reduce the paper flow between them. By eliminating purchasing orders for one whole product group, and introducing daily deliveries with monthly invoicing, it was possible to decrease the number of documents per transaction from seventeen to three. The potential for administrative savings may be seen in the example of the Skanska construction company, which receives more than 1.2 million supplier invoices annually. Internal calcula-tions indicate that it costs over Sw.Kr. 200 (£20) to handle each invoice.

In addition to administrative savings to be gained through closer co-operation with suppliers, many other costs are affected by corporate purchasing methods (see Figure 3.4).

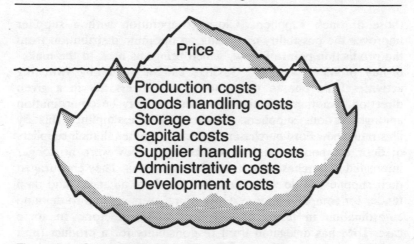

Figure 3.4 Costs affected by purchasing

Some of these costs are very visible ones (prices, rebates, etc.). Others are less tangible, but may none the less account for a large proportion of spending. Such indirect costs are very different depending on how the purchasing company chooses to work with its suppliers, and close co-operation with suppliers can bring such costs down substantially.

The main costs affected by purchasing method are:

1 Production costs
2 Goods handling costs
3 Storage costs
4 Capital costs
5 Supplier handling costs
6 Administrative costs
7 Development costs.

In relation to purchasing, these costs are considered indirect. Below, we discuss all the items listed above, with the exception of item 7, which is addressed in the section on development through supplier relations. We consider items 2–4 as one group, referring to them as materials flow costs, and items 5–6 as a group referred to as handling costs.

Lower production costs

One tangible way of reducing production costs is to take advantage of the possibilities of combining in-house production activities with those of one's suppliers. Close co-operation with a supplier improves the possibility of finding an optimum distribution from the production point of view, which brings us back to the make-or-buy problem complex. Savings can be made by switching activities from one to the other – not necessarily in a given direction. Another effectiveness measure may be co-ordination amongst various suppliers. Marier (1989) exemplifies this by illustrating how Ford purchasers collected together all their suppliers of door components and announced that they were no longer interested in purchasing individual components. They encouraged their suppliers to do what they could to form alliances, and then tender for complete door systems. Purchasers could also demand co-ordination in terms of suppliers' subcontractors. In some cases IBM has delegated total responsibility for a product (unit sourcing) to one supplier to whom IBM supplies some components and demands that all other suppliers be approved by them. In summary, we appear to be moving towards production networks in which a large number of specialized production units are interconnected in order to achieve economies of integration. An important prerequisite for increasing production-system effectiveness in this way is a new view of the material flow between companies. In order to accept this view, we must examine cost items 2–4 in the list of cost components given above.

Lower materials flow costs

Materials flow costs include goods handling, storage, and capital costs. These costs may be the ones which receive most attention in discussions of efficiency measures and close supplier relations. Many firms have achieved substantial effectiveness savings by reducing their stores of input goods and their intermediate stores in the production process, with the Japanese automotive industry as a source of inspiration. At one such industry, visiting Westerners made the following comment in the early 1980s:

It only takes 10 minutes inside an assembly plant in Japan to realize that relationships with suppliers are very different. The visitor accustomed to the loading docks, the large storage areas and the large incoming inspection area, typical of US plants, is likely to be taken aback by the stocking of Japanese assembly lines. Trucks from suppliers back up through large bay doors right to the assembly line; supplier personnel unload a few hours of parts, clean up the area and depart. There is no incoming inspection, no staging area, no expediting of material, just a seemingly continuous flow of material.

(Abernathy and Clark 1982: 8)

This philosophy, referred to as JIT, is considered the main factor underlying the competitive power of Japanese firms (Gadde and Grant 1984 and Ikeda 1987). Thus it has been natural for other automobile manufacturers to try to neutralize this competitive edge. It is equally natural for other purchasing-intensive companies with similar supply situations to try to emulate these ideas, and there are many successful examples. Raia (1988) claims that Chrysler's early, extensive JIT initiatives were one of the main factors contributing to its recovery after the crisis of the early 1980s. Increasing the efficiency of materials flow reduced the tied-up capital by more than one billion dollars.

The ideas behind JIT purchasing have spread like wildfire. One American study indicates that 87 per cent of the respondent companies either had well-developed or recently initiated programmes for JIT purchasing (Gilbert 1990).

Another American study analysed the effects for twenty purchasing companies which had introduced JIT deliveries (Dion *et al*. 1990). These firms had been using JIT for an average of 4.2 years. The frequency of deliveries had increased by an average of 200 per cent, and there were substantial positive effects. Lead times had dropped by over 40 per cent, and complaints reduced by the same amount. On the whole, it was found that purchaser complaints about product supplies were 20 to 30 per cent lower for JIT-supplied products than for products supplied in other ways.

Although much of the savings for large assembly firms has been in reduction in tied-up capital, many other types of cost savings have been made by other kinds of firms where goods-handling costs have proved to be the main source of potential cost reductions. For instance, in a collaboration project between the SIAB construction company and the materials producer Rockwool, handling costs at construction sites were found to be nearly 40 per cent of the purchase price for insulation products when using a traditional working method. Through changes in the packaging system, in combination with a new unloading system, it was possible to reduce these costs by two-thirds. In other words, in this case, collaboration between supplier and customer led to the design of a new handling system based on changes in both the supplier's and customer's organizations. Inspection or incoming control may also be extremely costly, for example, for firms which need large quantities of high-quality raw materials (such as pharmaceuticals or agricultural products). Agreements between such a firm and its suppliers, leaving the firm's incoming control procedures to the supplier who supplies a product the inspection of which is guaranteed, may make it possible to eliminate one needless control step entirely.

The main effects achieved have been in terms of tied-up capital, and are a result of decreased inventories. Figure 3.5 presents changes in the average amounts of tied-up capital in the 1970s and 1980s for seventy Swedish companies traded on the stock exchange. On the average, they freed one-third of their capital, mainly as the result of changes in purchasing behaviour.

Some of these effects were achieved by decreasing the number of suppliers. Undoubtedly, this new view of the usefulness of a consistent, well-thought-out supplier structure is here to stay. The obvious advantage of more efficient materials flows and the possibility of impacting on administrative costs have proved to be more important than the independence which was previously considered a key issue. Some firms have introduced administrative sanctions for units which take on new suppliers. There have been internal fines of up to Sw.Kr. 50,000 (£5,000). Others carry out effectiveness measurements using number of suppliers and changes in supplier structure as parameters.

Lower handling costs

Any customer–supplier relationship generates a number of documents. The costs for production and handling of these documents and other administrative activities may be an important element of a relationship. The traditional method of purchasing led to firms using large numbers of suppliers. Major construction companies may have tens of thousands of suppliers on their ledgers. In 1987, the city of Stockholm had more than 15,000. By reducing the number of suppliers, resources can be freed for investment in deeper relations with the remaining ones.

Handling costs in relation to suppliers may also be affected

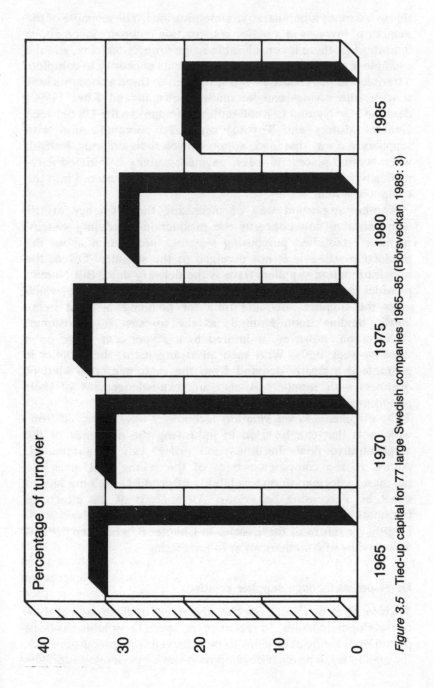

Figure 3.5 Tied-up capital for 77 large Swedish companies 1965–85 (Börsveckan 1989: 3)

through various administrative simplifications. The example of the number of invoices in a major construction company given above indicates that there is considerable scope for economizing, and the example in which the number of documents necessary to complete a transaction was reduced from seventeen to three also shows how considerable savings can be made. Newman and Rhee (1990) describe how Nummi (a joint venture company in the US between General Motors and Toyota) organized communication with suppliers in a way that made supplier invoices superfluous. Instead, when Nummi places an order, payment activity is initiated automatically, as all information on the transaction is entered into the computer system.

Another important way of increasing the efficiency of the administrative flow concerns the production-scheduling system. In most established purchasing systems, information about the production schedule is not divulged to the supplier. Often, the only information suppliers have is the delivery date. But Nummi provides suppliers with a forecast for nine weeks in advance, which gives the supplier adequate time for planning, without being legally binding upon Nummi, as the forecast is provisional. Its variation, however, is limited to a 20-per-cent range on a week-by-week basis. With such an arrangement, the supplier is guaranteed a steady demand from the customer. This kind of openness with suppliers is also an acknowledgement of their importance (Newman and Rhee 1990).

Developments in information technology have provided firms with tools that can be used in improving the efficiency of the administrative flow. Inquiries and orders can be automated. Access to the computer system of the selling firm gives the purchaser information on availability of products, helping him to adapt his purchasing behaviour. An analysis of the effects of information technology on purchasing is found in Dubois *et al.* (1989). We return to these issues in Chapter 8, where we present an overview of communication in purchasing.

Development through supplier relations

We have already pointed out the advantages of close co-operation on development issues. In recent years, special emphasis has been placed on the efficiency gains to be achieved through cutting back the lead times in product development work by coupling suppliers into the process at an earlier stage (see, e.g., Hay 1988, Burt 1989, and Takeuchi and Nonaka 1986). It is also possible to make quality assurance activities, which are an essential part of production, more effective through activating suppliers.

The Japanese automobile manufacturers have worked differently from their Western colleagues in this respect as well. Hervey (1982) pointed out that one consequence of a more concentrated supplier structure and greater openness was close technological collaboration in product development and design. Hervey sees this as an important competitive advantage for the Japanese automobile manufacturers. Furthermore, developments have meant that today a car contains components from a large number of technological fields, and it is difficult for individual companies to maintain sufficient in-house competence in all these areas. In this way, the composition of a car has changed, moving away from iron and steel in the direction of more electronics, plastics and light metals. In light of this, it was no surprise in the early 1980s when the automobile manufacturers of the Western world made a joint statement that they were in favour of putting development work more and more in the hands of the suppliers in order to purchase complete subsystems themselves, instead of components (see Gadde and Grant 1984).

To make it possible to purchase complete systems from independent suppliers, there must be close co-operation between buyer and seller. Purchase of components and systems developed externally must be co-ordinated both in-house and in relation to other suppliers. There must be close co-operation with a supplier before the supplier is contracted to do development work and take responsibility for a system. The purchaser must first be assured that the supplier has sufficient expertise and resources to succeed with the assignment.

In such development work, too, suppliers may be an important resource. Firms which take advantage of their suppliers' expertise may improve the effectiveness of their own product-development processes. Eriksson and Håkansson (1990) have shown that it is possible to come a long way in this respect. They report on two cases where purchasing firms have developed new products through systematic collaboration with suppliers. Both companies engaged a number of suppliers to solve crucial technical problems for them. In other words, there is good reason for a purchasing firm to involve suppliers in their own development work, and to become involved in the corresponding activities of their suppliers.

Other examples are provided by Raia (1991). Rank Xerox has shortened its product-development time by more than half. One important factor in this process was that suppliers were encouraged to make suggestions on how to improve quality, reduce lead times and cut costs. In addition to dramatic improvements of product quality, direct material costs were reduced by 75 per cent and the total manufacturing lead time for new products was reduced from nine months to less than two. Other companies are also reported to have adopted a similar teamwork approach to product development. Ford works with selected suppliers from the beginning, offering five-year contracts in return for assistance in the early design phase. Ingersoll-Rand brought in a plastics moulder and a couple of other key suppliers when a new air-grinder was only 'a gleam in the eye of the marketing manager' (Raia 1991: 39).

PROBLEMS ASSOCIATED WITH CHANGING SUPPLIER RELATIONS

In the previous section, we illustrated the intentions of purchasing firms with regard to quality improvements in supplier relations. We also gave examples of activities and measures implemented by individual firms to bring about these changes. Below, we discuss some experience of the effects of such measures.

Problems in taking the rationalization route

Above, we described the advantages of the introduction of JIT deliveries, and pointed out that many companies have invested heavily in building up such supply systems.

Experience shows very clearly that the transition to JIT is far from simple. Stundza (1985) has shown the distinct problems experienced by Chrysler in the mid-1980s in attempting to get its JIT system functioning satisfactorily. Harbour (1986) reported on a study visit at a new hi-tech unit; the company could demonstrate that supplies arrived on schedule, but on the shop floor the impression of the whole was entirely different.

But when I walked through the plant I saw weeks of stampings, acres of work-in-process, and subassemblies strewn around the body-shop. Boxes of parts were stacked so high on the chassis and trim lines, that it was difficult to see what was going on in those areas. In fact, the inventory took up so much room that they could have put five major press lines in the same space. 'This is JIT,' I wondered?

(Harbour 1986: 14)

It is interesting to compare this quote with the one describing impressions from Japan. It is clear that JIT must not only be seen as a materials supply system. In reality it is one of the main components of an integrated production system. Without this kind of coupling to production, sub-deliveries of the JIT type might lead to poorer effectiveness of material supply than with previously applied principles. In the study by Dion *et al.* (1990) referred to above, it was found that there were two main problems that had to be solved in order to create a functioning system. One was ensuring the quality of the product before it entered the customer's production system, the other was co-ordinating the buyer's demand for deliveries with the supplier's rate of production.

The initial effect of this latter problem was that inventory was moved to an earlier stage in the production chain. This was found, for example, by Nishiguchi (1989) in a comparative study of JIT in Japan, Europe and the US, and a study by Hutchins (1986) of Rank Xerox. In the American automobile industry, Raia (1988) observed that delivery frequency from suppliers increased, which was one of the ambitions underlying this new way of thinking. However, these deliveries often came from newly established warehouses. One firm even picked the name 'JIT-Warehousing'. The inventory business in Detroit flourished. Zipkin (1991) reported corresponding effects, and found that JIT gave rise to a number of unpleasant confrontations between customers and suppliers. Such problems were not expected to arise, as suppliers were, in turn, meant to develop JIT systems for their own production and in-deliveries. Establishing links into a total JIT system in this way is a highly demanding process. Toyota began experimenting with its system in 1948. A few years later, it had, in principle, eliminated intermediate inventories in its own production process. It took seventeen more years before a fully synchronized system between Toyota and its first-tier suppliers had been established, and a further fifteen years before JIT had been established between first-tier suppliers and second-tier subcontractors. Not until the late 1980s were the very first steps taken towards including third-tier subcontractors in the Toyota system (Nishiguchi 1987).

We conclude that efforts to increase effectiveness in material supplies require extensive changes, and comprise a process in which many in-house measures must be implemented both by the purchasing firm and the supplier. Isolated efforts to increase delivery frequency from the purchasing side will not lead to effectiveness benefits unless they are combined with changes in the production system. The JIT strategy leads both to increased interdependence of various in-house company functions and increased dependence on external suppliers.

Problems in conjunction with the developmental role

Here, too, we find substantial time lags between ambitions and achieved effects. In the opinion of Burt and Sukoup (1985), in the mid 1980s the development potential of suppliers was completely unexploited by purchasers. They considered this an enormous strategic error.

Håkansson (1989) indicates that development collaboration is still a relatively unexploited resource. In a study of a large number of small and medium-sized firms, he found that, while more than one-fourth of these firms had had no development co-operation at all with any suppliers during the three-year period prior to the study, 15 per cent of the firms co-operated on development with more than five of their suppliers. Why would one out of every four manufacturing firms have no development co-operation at all with suppliers? One explanation is that there are still many companies which have not realized the potential of close co-operation with their suppliers. It is also important to clarify that, although up to this point we have only analysed the benefits of this type of collaboration from the purchasing firm's point of view, there must be mutual interest in order for such co-operation to take place. Collaboration should be of interest to suppliers as well, as it would give them the opportunity to be more closely coupled to their customers, a marketing strategy which has proved to be highly advantageous (Hammarkvist *et al.* 1982). Still, some suppliers might hesitate, because this type of market investment has more than a revenue side to it, and may both be extremely expensive and experienced as risky. Within the framework of traditional forms of payment and agreements, a supplier is not paid for his efforts until supply of the finished goods to the purchaser has begun. In light of this, it is natural that the inclination of the supplier to become involved in development projects would be conditioned by the previous behaviour of the purchasing firm. It is reasonable to imagine that the price-pressure strategy described above as previously prevailing on the purchaser side would increase supplier hesitancy. If an individual supplier's share of the buyer's business is going to go on fluctuating from year to year, depending on its resistance in the playoffs conducted by the purchaser, it will be difficult, if not impossible, for a supplier to make the relevant calculations for such an investment.

CONCLUSIONS

In this chapter, we have seen the changes in purchasing firms' behaviour. Their degree of vertical integration has decreased, owing to increased specialization. This has meant that 'buy' has become a more important strategy than 'make'. In order to make purchasing more effective, and to integrate it into the production system, purchasing firms have identified a need to change the organization of their supplier structures. Closer co-operation with a smaller number of suppliers has made it possible to improve efficiency considerably, both in relation to rationalization and development. We have also shown that although there are substantial potential effects these may be difficult to achieve, or at least that the process takes time.

In summary, we can state that there has been considerably increased effectiveness in materials handling and, in many cases, substantial profits have been made. Still, there are many examples of failures, and even investments which have now proved to be fruitful have been riddled with problems of implementing the new ways of thinking. In these examples, the mistake that has been made throughout is that the parties involved have not realized the degree of reciprocal dependence required in the entire chain, from design and development of a product to use. The product absorbs costs throughout the process, and the only way of reducing this absorption is to change, i.e. to reduce, either time, processes or handling operations – for the entire chain. In some situations, changes can also be made by transferring operations, but this normally leads to much smaller savings than doing away with them altogether.

With regard to the development role, it is a prerequisite for increased involvement from the supplier that some kind of guarantee be given that the business will be of a sufficiently long-term nature to make it reasonably certain that development costs will be met. Berry (1982) found that in the past purchasers often turned to a competitor of the supplier who was doing the development work and placed an order for the same component so as to have an alternative. The kind of change buyers now desire to bring about clearly implies demands for new kinds of relations and new kinds of business agreements between buyer and seller.

To achieve this, there will have to be an open relation between customer and supplier, resulting in the suppliers' being given a reasonable product specification, so that they do not 'overdevelop' in relation to what is needed. This also requires a change of attitude on the part of the purchasing company with regard to the significance they attribute to the various criteria for purchasing. And last but not least, this change has to be communicated to the supplier, in order to impact on his involvement.

One cause of the difficulties found with respect to application of the new way of thinking about purchasing is that there is altogether too much focus by the purchasing firm on its own operations. If the potential improvements are to be realized, the problem cannot be seen solely as one of purchasing strategy. For the buyer to raise the quality of supplier relations, internal changes must come first. Only after that can his suppliers be encouraged to change. We have seen that the process of change may work poorly if the problems are viewed only from the perspective of the purchasing firm. For this reason, we need to analyse the characteristics of a customer–supplier relation; Chapter 4 is devoted to a discussion of typical features of well-developed supplier relations. The present chapter has also concluded that, owing to the reciprocal nature of the work of various companies, individual supplier relations cannot be seen in isolation from other supplier relations. In Chapter 5 supplier networks are analysed.

Chapter 4

Supplier relations

As indicated in the discussions above, there is a relationship, or connection, between a buyer and each of the individual suppliers. The first three chapters also provided an overview of a fundamental change, in which purchasing companies have gradually been making a transition from 'looser' to 'more solid' connections. Because the concept of 'solid' connections is far from simple or homogeneous, we devote this chapter to a discussion and analysis of some of its central elements. This chapter is divided into eight sections. The first section characterizes supplier relationships, and identifies six of their specific features, to each of which a subsequent section is devoted. The first of these features is the complexity of these relationships in terms of the multifaceted contacts between the companies. The second is the long-term nature of the relationship, which often stretches over decades, and the third is the scope of adaptation of individual relationships required, from both the technological and organizational points of view. A fourth main characteristic, because it emphasizes the informal nature of the relationship, is the low degree of formalization, indicating that the firms do their best to safeguard themselves against unpleasant surprises through reciprocal trust rather than through formal agreements. The fifth characteristic is the power/dependence balance in the relationship, and the sixth and final one is the simultaneous presence of conflict and co-operation, with one conclusion being that effective relationships must contain elements of both.

GENERAL CHARACTERISTICS OF BUYER–SELLER RELATIONSHIPS

Business transactions between buyers and sellers may differ greatly from one another. At one end of the spectrum there are simple deals in which a person from the buying firm has a limited number of contacts with a person from the selling firm, and in which the products and conditions of their discussion are virtually standardized. At the other, a large number of officials representing several functions at the buying firm have contacts with officials in corresponding positions at the selling firm. In this case a large number of technical, administrative, and economic problems are ventilated.

Every business transaction is an interesting phenomenon in itself. We use the term 'episode' to define this type of event, limited in time. Many things which can happen between a buyer and seller such as a joint development project, testing a new product, or re-negotiating a long-term contract, can comprise an episode. How each episode is handled will depend first on how complex the episode is in itself, and second on the history of the previous relationship between the parties. They may already have met in many past episodes, and have developed an existing relationship.

The way the current episode is handled will depend largely on the past history. If the parties have come to trust one another, the situation will be handled differently from the way it will if the opposite applies. In other words, actions in given situations must not be seen in isolation, but must be viewed and understood in the light of previous occurrences.

For these reasons, it is important to base an analysis of upcoming actions on the complexity of past episodes, and the degree to which the relationship has already developed. Table 4.1 may be seen as a point of departure for discussing what happens when these two dimensions are combined.

Table 4.1 Business transactions: four cases

	No previous relationship	Well-developed relationship
Simple episode	Case 1	Case 2
Complex episode	Case 3	Case 4

If there is no previous relationship, behaviour within the episode will be complete unto itself, and thus has to be judged and optimized as if it were to remain an isolated episode. If, as in case 1, the episode is a simple one, a typical market situation arises in which both parties are truly independent and may even be previously unknown to one another. Taking such an episode to its extreme, it may even be mediated via an exchange market. There is no past history and no likelihood that the transaction will lead to the initiation of a relationship.

Every company has purchases which fall under case 1. These may be highly standardized raw materials, or very simple products purchased in small amounts.

If the episode is a complex one in itself, a different situation arises (case 3). Complexity generates uncertainty. For this kind of business transaction to be completed, for example, when a company is going to buy a non-standard product from a new supplier, the episode must be handled in such a way as to build up sufficient trust between the parties. The experience gained when a complex episode is carried out may lead to the creation of some kind of relationship between the two parties involved, and this may impact on their future interaction. For this reason, case 3 is of special interest, as a typical first episode which may lead to an established relationship, and which gives both parties a good opportunity to get to know one another.

Case 3 may also be a one-off purchase, for instance, when a firm buys a piece of equipment which is not normally part of its plant. Large investments also have these characteristics, even when the parties have been in contact previously. Such episodes are so large and unique that the past relationship becomes relatively less significant. However, there are still rules applying to technical relationships which make it better for the purchasing firm to work with suppliers from whom they have bought in the past.

When there is an established relationship (cases 2 and 4), each individual transaction always has to be seen in relation to it. As a rule, the relationship facilitates individual episodes, which should be formulated so as to strengthen the relationship. In other words, how each episode is structured in relation to previous and anticipated episodes is more important than the fact that it is well formulated in itself. This is particularly important in relation to complex episodes. This connection between individual episodes and the long-term relationship means both considerable simplification of day-to-day work and the establishment of a dependency relation. One way in which the complexity becomes visible is that a number of officials at each firm are in contact with one another over time. In other words, the relationship consists of a number of intertwined, interdependent connections at the individual level, which require special efforts to handle.

A second important trait of relationships, as pointed out above, is that they are of a long-term nature. A relationship comprises a number of episodes and, in some cases, has a protective, strengthening function, for instance when there are tensions among the parties involved. At the same time, in other situations, the existence of a relationship may impose limitations, for example when one of the firms wants to implement rapid changes. The very fact that a relationship is, by nature, a long-term undertaking, means that it has pros and cons. One way of elucidating this long-term characteristic is to see a relationship as an investment which, in terms of resources, makes it comparable to machinery or equipment used over a long period of time.

One vital aspect of the relationship's being long term is that both parties adapt. Many adaptations are conscious and considered, while others happen more automatically, as a result of the complexity in the course of events described above. Handling of adaptations is important in several respects, as it can either give rise to blocks or enable skill and development potential to be used to advantage. Moreover, adaptations can be made in different dimensions: product and/or production technology, administration, knowledge, or economic aspects.

Furthermore, relationships are social processes in which different types of confidence-building activities are extremely important. It is impossible to cover all conceivable issues in agreements and contracts. There must be space in which informal, personal one-to-one contact takes over.

There are stages in the process of a relationship in which each party – the buyer and the seller – plays the key role in relation to the other, and in which situations of more or less strong dependence take over. Dependence carries power in its wake, and thus it is very important, and often extremely difficult, to handle a relationship in terms of power and dependence. The power/dependence relationship is often an asymmetrical one, and also shifts with time owing, *inter alia*, to the general state of the economy.

Finally, it is important to see that a relationship has other aspects to it besides co-operation. There will always be conflicting interests, which give rise to tension. One important attribute of effective relationships is that such conflicts are not suppressed, but allowed to surface and then to be handled constructively.

In the coming sections, the attributes identified above, the complexity, long-term nature, adaptability, informal social processes and power/dependence, as well as the existence of conflict and co-operation in relationships, will be discussed one by one. When we do this, it is important to keep in mind that relationships are entities, and their holistic nature implies that they do not easily succumb to being classified into different dimensions. We consider these classifications useful primarily from a pedagogical point of view.

COMPLEXITY

In one of our studies, there was a supplier relationship in which roughly 600 people in the purchasing firm were in regular, significant contact with no fewer than 200 people in the selling firm. This extreme case gives some indication of the complexity of relationships in terms of sheer numbers of people involved. At another large mechanical engineering company, the purchasing manager admitted that he had held his position for a whole year before learning that two large meetings were held annually at which the technicians at his firm met with the technicians from one of their main suppliers and discussed technical issues. Apparently, since the technicians thought that 'no commercial issues were discussed' at these meetings, they did not see any reason to involve the purchasing department. These examples indicate that, in many cases, there are extensive contacts with many officials from various departments on both sides meeting to discuss and solve more or less advanced problems. Even if these problems are solved independently of one another, though, this does not mean that they are independent. Rather, they are interconnected in many ways, and improved contacts between the firms would undoubtedly be very important. Figure 4.1 depicts the complexity that may be found in an extensive relationship.

Thus it can be seen that a particular extensive relationship may be highly complex, and require substantial co-ordination of operations at the purchasing firm. One interesting solution, seldom applied today, is appointing a specific person to manage co-ordination of a given supplier relationship. At many firms the purchaser fulfils this function indirectly, but as he is concurrently responsible both for many suppliers and other tasks as well, it is often not possible for him to be an effective co-ordinator in practice.

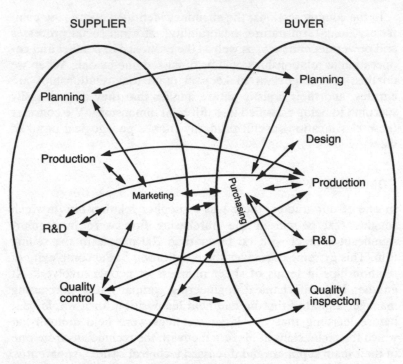

Figure 4.1   Pattern of contacts in an advanced supplier relationship

The complexity of personal contacts and patterns of communication discussed above is, of course, attributable to complexity at a deeper level, relating to dependence with regard to each individual supplier relationship, and the interdependence among them. First, there is dependence in relation to the way the production technology, logistics and administration of the purchasing firm work. All supplier relationships have to be coordinated with regard to the technical and organizational resources of the purchasing firm. The solution found in relation to one supplier also affects this function in other relationships as well, which means that solving a problem with regard to one relationship may give rise to consequent problems in others.

Second, the relationship of the purchasing firm with supplier A may be contingent on how well relations with supplier B or customer C work, and vice versa, i.e. the purchasing firm may use its relationship with A to affect a third party. This means, for example, that the purchasing firm may discuss a technical development project with one supplier in order to get that supplier to behave in a certain way in relation to another party the buying firm wishes to affect. The more concentrated the network the individual firm works within, the more elaborate this type of behaviour has to be.

The type of complexity related to co-ordination of an individual relationship with others is considerably more difficult to handle than the type of complexity which arises with regard to co-ordination within one relationship. This is because there is an infinite number of ways of implementing the former type of co-ordination, and a conspicuous absence of simple solutions. It should be an appropriate first step to have the executives in the purchasing department identify the main connections and then, in systematic discussions with other executives, raise the awareness both of the current and the potential connections, so that they will both respect and take advantage of the opportunities arising from various situations.

Generally, we find that the complexity of the supplier relation can be explained by the fact that the 'coupling' in the relationship is complex in itself from a technical, organizational and social point of view, i.e. a large number of officials are involved. This in turn creates a large number of problems of communication and co-ordination. Secondly, the complexity is attributable to the fact that there is dependence on other relations. We return to these problems and the possibilities for dealing with them in Chapter 5.

RELATIONSHIPS AS INVESTMENTS – THEIR LONG-TERM NATURE

One very important element of relationships is that they are of a long-term nature. Deep relationships are often decades old. In other words, there is always a history which affects and is affected by the current interplay. Furthermore, there are often more or less overtly expressed expectations. Every action in a relationship must, therefore, be seen in a time perspective. Table 4.2 illustrates the relevant kind of time dimension by recapitulating the duration pattern of a number of supplier relationships for technical development (Håkansson 1989).

One of the classic ways of accounting for the time dimension in economics is to examine activities with long-term effects as if they were investments. The difference between an investment and a

Table 4.2 Duration of supplier relationships for technical development

Duration	Proportion of relationships (%)
0–4 years	28
5–14 years	41
>15 years	29
Weighted average	13 years

Source: Håkansson 1989: 112

cost, in principle, is that the revenue accruing from them is expected to take different courses in time. An investment is made on one occasion (in one period of time), and is expected to provide return over several periods, while a cost is associated with an activity the return on which is expected to come during the same period.

If we begin by examining the costs in a supplier relationship, we find that there are many items, and that they can mainly be divided into two groups: contact/information costs and adaptation costs. The contact/information costs of a relationship are high in the initial stages, when the buyer is getting to know the suppliers and their abilities and expertise, and these costs fall later. During certain later episodes contacts may need to be supplemented, which is associated with short-term additional costs, but generally the lower cost level may be maintained. Adaptation costs are all of a one-off nature, but as they arise successively, there is some natural adaptation over time, although there is a tendency for them to crop up early in a relationship. All the elementary adaptations necessary for the buyer to use the supplier must be made initially, which means that neither of the two main categories of costs is evenly distributed over time, and that the introductory period is liable to be a costly one.

We have discussed revenues which result from relationships above. Such revenues may include rationalization benefits or contributions to technical development. Some benefits (such as price benefits) may occur from the very first day, while many others, such as development benefits, take time. Studies made to date indicate that for two parties to venture to take the step of initiating joint development work, they need to have a long shared history. In other words, the return on a relationship also changes over time, but in the other direction, compared with costs.

If we examine the cost and revenue aspects in overview,

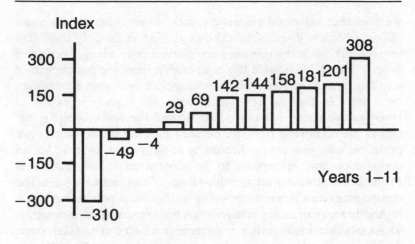

Profits per year

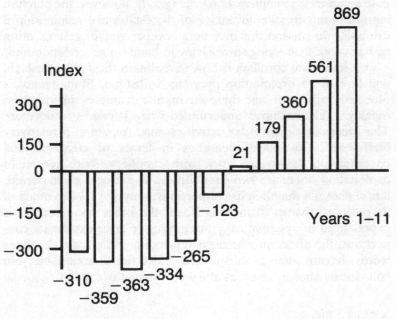

Accumulated profits

Figure 4.2 Cost/revenue structure in customer–supplier relationships

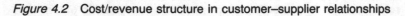

we find that relationships very clearly have some of the same characteristics as investments. The costs arise in an early stage (the investment), while the revenues are accrued over a longer period of time. Figure 4.2 illustrates this relationship from the perspective of a selling firm. The figure shows changes in customer profitability over time. In the first few years, costs are slightly in excess of revenues, which do not exceed costs until the fourth year. If the figures are accumulated, it can be seen that the relationship is not profitable until year seven. According to this report, from an Italian consultancy firm, it appears to be more effective to retain and maintain old customer relationships than to seek out new ones. The cost/revenue distribution is probably similar for a purchasing firm.

Another way of seeing relationships with regard to investments is to ask whether a relationship is a resource which can be taken over. The answer is not completely clear. It is difficult to transfer a relationship to some other unit. If a firm acquires another firm, and somehow takes over operations, relationships may come along as part of the package. This is not necessarily simply an advantage, as it may pose an obstacle to implementing changes. If, however, the purchasing firm wants to take advantage of the established relationship it can easily do so, and this may be a cheaper way of getting into a new network than trying successively to build up new relationships.

One important corollary is how to maintain these relationships, and how much exploitation they can withstand. Maintenance is obviously important, and there are infinite examples showing how quickly a relationship is undermined when it ceases to develop. This means that day-to-day activities must remain at a relatively high level. This places demands in terms of creativity and continuity in day-to-day work with suppliers. With regard to exploitation, there are two possibilities. If, during a given period, a firm does not maintain its connections, it may still keep much of its position, thanks to inertia. If, on the other hand, a firm is experienced as systematically attempting to over-exploit its connections, the effect may be both very rapid and painful. In other words, having some problems and difficulties is acceptable, but consciously abusing one's established connections is not.

ADAPTATIONS

Adaptation is one of the characteristic phenomena associated with relationships. In principle, adaptation in a relationship means that a certain supplier is handled in a unique way, either to give lower total costs or to give that supplier priority in relation to others. If all the parties involved – suppliers or customers – looked identical, purchased the same volumes and quantities, and had the same technological structure, adaptation would be irrelevant. Thus the degree of adaptation stands in direct proportion to the differences between the parties: the greater the differences the greater reason to make specific adaptations, and these may be seen as the means available to a firm to take advantage of the unique attributes of its supplier. By discovering and making use of these unique attributes, the purchasing firm may achieve a number of positive effects.

For instance, some specific attributes may be associated with the technology used by the supplier. Various suppliers may use the same technology and thus have some of the same attributes. Consequently, some adaptations may mean that a firm adapts not to a single supplier but to a certain category of supplier, with interchangeable members.

We now go on to discuss three particular aspects of adaptation. First we describe and exemplify various types of adaptation: technical, knowledge-based, administrative, economic and legal. Second, we analyse the way adaptations take place by distinguishing major adaptations occurring on isolated occasions from gradual, incremental adaptations over time. Third, we discuss some of the factors affecting the demand for and content of adaptations, primarily those relating to the technological structure of the firms and products concerned.

There are many types of adaptations. This has been shown in our previous discussions of effectiveness measures and elsewhere. One very important type is the technical ones. Buyers and sellers on industrial markets have plants and equipment with specific technical attributes, and their relationships are intended to bind them to one another effectively. Naturally, this places demands on and opens potential for technological adaptations, both in terms of the product sold by the supplier and the product manufactured by the buyer, as well as in terms of the production processes of each. In one large study we found that the purchasing firms primarily had technological co-operation with materials suppliers (Håkansson 1989). In other words, materials adaptations appeared to be the most common type of adaptations, and we found this somewhat surprising. It may be explained by the fact that, from a production point of view, input goods are often the main cost factor. Of course we also found a number of adaptations regarding components and equipment.

Knowledge-based adaptations gain in importance the more development issues are emphasized in supplier relationships. In this respect as well, one may easily speak in terms of the necessity for a purchasing firm to market its needs. Buyers who encourage their suppliers to increase their knowledge of the buyer's application of technology, give themselves an important developmental boost. But in doing so the purchasing firm also commits itself, as it becomes better and better at using the technology of the supplier in question. Thus two bases of knowledge, that of the buyer and that of the supplier, proceed to approach one another, with reciprocal adaptation. Probably they should not be allowed to become too similar. There is some advantage in retaining a modicum of 'friction', as the differences between them become a point of departure for future developments. This potential may be more positive if the two units remain separate.

There may also be adaptations of administrative routines. Planning, supply and communications systems may need to be adapted so the firms can work together effectively. Chapter 8 provides a number of examples of how firms have developed joint communications systems.

Such adaptations take the form both of major one-off measures and small, successive steps over time. As a rule, major adaptations are highly visible ones which the parties involved consider strategic, while smaller adaptations are handled 'locally' in the organization, and are considered natural measures necessary to facilitate collaboration. Frequently, such adaptations are substantial, although this may not be evident until one of the parties want to implement a major change. The size and value of these successive adaptations are thus often difficult to overview, and there is a general tendency to underestimate their significance.

The need for adaptation will clearly depend on the attributes of the two parties. First, the need may arise because of specific characteristics of the seller, for example if the seller is a foreign company the buyer may demand local warehousing or some kind of local service. Second, the need may arise because of unique demands made by the purchasing firm. These may come up because the buyer is, in turn, subjected to unique demands from his customers or is working under special conditions for some other reason. Thirdly, the combination of seller and buyer and their interaction may create both demands and potential for specific adaptations.

The nature of these adaptations also depends on the type of product involved. Some products (such as some equipment) are routinely adapted, while others (such as material and standard components) tend to appear in standardized versions. Some customers purchase in such volumes that supply and inventory adaptations are important, while others (such as materials supplies) may be marked by considerable variation in both content and volume, making administrative adaptation of interest. This implies that product type and adaptation type are closely interrelated.

RECIPROCAL TRUST RATHER THAN FORMALITY

One of the things that characterizes business deals is that they always contain uncertainty. Some of this is about the future, and is genuine, i.e. it can never be reduced, only handled with more or less sophisticated assessments. Other aspects of insecurity are directly related to the other party in the transaction. For example, there is often a time lag between the transaction itself and the delivery. In addition, it is impossible to specify or measure all the functions or characteristics of a product, even at a specific delivery. Instead, they become visible gradually. Unexpected events may also mean that the content of the business deal must be adjusted, and the technology may be both complex and difficult to assess in advance. Thus there are a number of factors which are difficult to overview at the point when the deal is made. These difficulties are so great that it is often pointless – or far too costly – to try to formulate agreements to cover all conceivable situations. Instead, the relationship has to provide the security. Table 4.3 demonstrates that the degree of formalization in a relationship is generally low and, even when the relationship has developed to include substantial technical development, this is only established to a limited extent through formal agreements.

Security in a relationship cannot be created on a single occasion, but must develop over time. The connection must be built up through a process of interaction in which reciprocal trust can successively be deepened. Interaction may lead to the development of a learning process in which both sides gradually get a better idea of the situations in which it is suitable to do business.

Table 4.3 Use of formal contracts in supplier/customer relationships
involving technical development

Type of relationship	Customer relationships	Supplier relationships
Formal	%	%
Annual contracts	20	11
Long-term contracts	13	8
Joint corporation	2	2
	35	21
Informal		
Ongoing relationship	51	67
Other informal pattern	14	12
	65	79
Totals	100	100

Source: Håkansson 1989: 113

The typical process follows a course in which the two parties first
test one another through small business deals,and then move along
to more complete deliveries. In addition to its being important to
get to know one's counterpart well, it is also important to facilitate
that party's learning about one's own operations. In other words,
it is important to create different types of social situations in which
the personnel in the functions needing contact with one another
get to know their counterparts and their problems. There is even
an example in which these contacts have been extended to
comprise all personnel at a given unit. In one particular case, a
supplier brought his whole staff to see a major customer so that
all those involved would gain understanding of the consequences
of delays, and failure to meet quality standards.

The benefits of and the need for personal contacts in building
up confidence cannot be too much stressed. This is often recommended from a marketing point of view, but it is certainly equally
important for purchasing. We might even claim that the personal-
contact network is one of the most important personnel resources,
and that it should therefore be taken into consideration in recruitment of purchasers.

What happens, then, in situations in which one of the parties
implements a measure which has a negative effect on the other?
The answer will depend on how the other side sees that measure.
If there are persuasive arguments for it, the dissatisfaction may be
short-lived, but if the measure is interpreted as a long-term change
of attitude, even a small shift may have grave consequences. This

is where personal contacts between individuals at both firms become most important, as these may serve to give the other party a far more complete picture of why a certain measure is necessary. With such a personal network, a relationship can withstand substantial strain occasionally if the underlying policy remains the same. However, even small changes may impact greatly on the relationship if they are interpreted as shifting this underlying position.

POWER AND DEPENDENCE

Power and dependence are important aspects of supplier relationships. At least for large firms, the most important supplier relationships always involve large volumes, and are thus the principal ones for both parties from an economic point of view. They also affect both parties in a number of indirect ways, which further increases their significance. Significance creates dependence, and the way in which the power/dependence issue is handled thus becomes an important aspect of purchasing work. In the past, it was recommended that purchasers should try to behave in such a way that dependence did not arise. Independence was a key objective. As purchasing has begun to work more systematically with long-term relationships, dependence is now more accepted, and the question has become how to handle the various dependence situations. We discuss this change in the way purchasing is viewed in greater detail in the final chapter.

One of the problems associated with power/dependence relationships is that they are seldom symmetrical. As a rule, they are unbalanced with regard to individual dimensions. For example, the relationship may be more important to the seller than to the buyer from a volume point of view, or vice versa. However, a certain amount of imbalance in one dimension may be set off against the equivalent but opposite imbalance in another dimension. If this is not the case, it is important for the buyer to attempt to create such imbalances. If a purchasing firm wishes to try to get priority from one supplier despite the fact that it is not one of that firm's major buyers, it must begin by trying to make itself interesting in some other way, for instance from a technical point of view. The firm must try to set off its volume disadvantage with some other advantage. This type of 'balancing act' is an important aspect of handling suppliers.

Another characteristic attribute of the power/dependence relationship is that it usually varies with the general state of the economy. The seller may have more power during a boom, as may the buyer when supply exceeds demand. It may be tempting to exploit this variation for short-term gain, and there are examples from the Swedish steel industry of such behaviour between manufacturers and wholesalers (Gadde 1978). But a firm which tries to take advantage of such opportunities runs the risk of reprisals. If a buyer abuses his position during a recession, his firm may very well suffer when an economic upswing ensues. Handling of pricing issues is very important in this respect. Klint (1985) describes how buyers and sellers of paper pulp built up reciprocal trust through their behaviour in different business cycles.

There are no simple solutions to recommend to the problem of imbalance in the power/dependence relationship arising, for instance, as a result of changes in the economy. It is not easy to say what the best strategy is in any individual case. Certainly, though, awareness of the problems and regular, systematic discussions are a first step towards learning to handle these questions better.

CONFLICT AND CO-OPERATION

The parties in a business relationship have both contradictory interests and shared ones. If they do not learn to deal with the contradictory ones, conflicts arise. In the classic model of purchasing, relationships have been fraught with conflict. One typical example is this subcontractor, who characterizes his customers in the automotive industry as follows:

> They are nasty, abusive and ugly. They would take a dime from a starving grandmother. They steal our innovations, they make uneconomic demands, like 'follow us around the globe and build plants near ours. We need good suppliers like you but if you can't do it we'll find somebody else'.
>
> (Helper 1986: 17)

There are an endless number of such examples, and both sellers and buyers have plenty of examples of dirty tricks they have played on one another, and they tend to blow their own trumpets about them. Needless to say, this type of behaviour does nothing to promote close relationships.

Reciprocal trust is a prerequisite for long-term relationships, adaptations, and joint investments. Realization of this fact led one representative of the automotive industry to make the following statement with regard to an essential change in existing relations:

> We need new relationships with what we have to think of as a family of suppliers. We need to throw off the old shackles of adversarial confrontation and work together in an enlightened era of mutual trust and confidence.
>
> (Berry 1982: 26)

The description and aspiration is so heavenly that it almost makes one want to close with an 'amen'. At the same time, it is probably an erroneous appraisal of the ideal content of collaboration and conflict in a relationship. Unfortunately, there are altogether too many people who believe that elimination of all conflict in a relationship is a prerequisite for developing new supplier relations. It is important to point out that this is a misunderstanding. Of course effective relationships require some collaboration, but they require an equal measure of conflict. Figure 4.3 depicts the ideal relationship.

The figure describes one dimension of collaboration and one of conflict. If the degree of both are low, the relationship will not be especially meaningful to either party – such relationships are characterized as marginal. If there is a high degree of conflict and a low degree of collaboration, the relationship will not work very

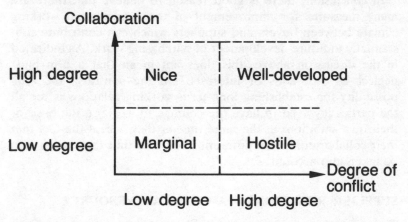

Figure 4.3 Relationships with different combinations of collaboration and conflict

well. Significant relationships come into being with a high degree of collaboration. A relationship with a low degree of conflict tends to be somewhat too 'nice'. The parties place too few demands on one another. Provided that it can be handled well, raising the degree of conflict in such a situation enables a better climate for innovation and development.

It seems that the desirable type of relationship is one in which conflict is handled constructively. In this, we agree with Gemünden (1985: 405) who says that 'buyer and seller should neither smooth over existing conflicts nor let them escalate'. There will be conflict as long as both parties remain independent, because they will never have identical goals. There will always be conflicts of interest between buyers and sellers, because there will always be the distribution problem: the profits generated by their joint work will have to be shared. This problem of distributing profits is mainly accentuated when their shared processing value falls. For these reasons, collaboration must continually develop so as to keep shared revenues at least at a constant level. Continuous development of collaboration to achieve 'mutual profits' or 'mutual success' (Hay 1988) is thus an effective way of preventing the escalation of conflict. Increased openness appears to be a prerequisite for this, particularly in relation to strategic issues. Expressions of this openness should include involving the supplier in the product-development process from an earlier stage than has previously been the case.

In conclusion, there is good reason to believe that there are many measures for improvement of the fundamental working climate between buyers and suppliers which can contribute substantially to future development of purchasing work. As indicated in the discussion above, this does not mean that a firm must neglect its own aims or interests. On the contrary, the only possibility for establishing long-term working relations is for all the parties involved to have the courage to work on the basis of their own ambitions at the same time as they accept the fact that their collaborators have different ones, and that these must also be taken into account.

SUPPLIER RELATIONS – A CRITICAL RESOURCE

The main characteristics of a firm's supplier relations are summarized below. Our first conclusion is that relationships with suppliers are very important. They have considerable economic impact, because such a large proportion of the firm's activities are channelled through them. As a rule, more than half of the total turnover of the firm (sometimes up to 70 per cent) is handled within these relationships. They are important from a technical point of view, as they integrate the technology of the purchasing company with that of the supplier. Consequently, they also become central from an innovative point of view. They are one of the most important interfaces at which the knowledge possessed by the firm encounters other large bodies of knowledge.

Secondly, supplier relations comprise major investments. It requires a great deal of work both to establish a relation and to adapt the firm to it internally. Consequently, well-established supplier relations is one of the most important resources any firm has.

Supplier relations are built up through human effort and human contacts. Thus, their third characteristic is that they are 'dynamic' in a number of respects. In order for them to survive, they must be under continual development. If they are not, there is a clear risk that one of the firms will develop the opinion that the other firm no longer considers the relationship important. The dynamic feature means both that all relations can be affected and that, in the long run, they are difficult to manipulate. Honesty is probably the word which recurs most frequently in our discussions with sellers and buyers of what characterizes good relations. Any sign of dishonesty has an immediately harmful effect on the relationship.

A fourth characteristic, to which we have thus far only alluded, is the fact that all the relationships a company has are interrelated and interdependent, and actually need to be seen as a network. The next chapter is devoted to this aspect of purchasing.

Chapter 5

Supplier networks

No relationship between two firms exists in a vacuum, independent of others. Material purchased from one supplier is used in equipment purchased from others. The more advanced the equipment, the more generally dependent it will be on the attributes of the material. Moreover, components which are going to be part of the same end product have to fit and work together. In other words, there are a number of obvious types of dependence among the purchased products. The adaptations discussed in the previous chapter lead to a gradual increase of this dependence. There may be adaptations to the selling firms technology, as well as in relation to other purchased products or services. In other words, not only are there given dependencies, but they are often systematically developed by the firms involved. Step by step, measures of a technical, administrative or logistical nature are implemented, where the use of one supplier is bound together with the use of certain others. Of course, how far this process goes will depend on how aware the firm is of the significance of this type of cost-influencing factor, and on whether the firm has conscious ambitions about keeping suppliers apart. Irrespective of the degree of awareness of these two issues, there will always be important dependencies amongst different suppliers. These relationships and what can be done to take systematic advantage of them is the focus of the present chapter.

WHAT IS UNIQUE ABOUT NETWORKS?

Let us use a basic definition to capture the unique quality of networks. A network is made up of inter-coupled connections (Cook and Emerson 1978). This means that if a change occurs in one relationship it will also affect others. Such couplings may be both positive and negative, so if a relationship takes a turn for the better (such as increased volumes) it will have a positive effect on others (their volumes may also increase) or a negative one (their volumes may decrease).

The existence of these couplings is absolutely essential. They give a firm many opportunities to affect others indirectly, i.e. via someone else. For example, if a firm wants to affect supplier A, it may first try direct impact, but if this fails it may be able to affect A via someone else – another customer, a consultancy firm, a supplier of A's, etc. Furthermore, these couplings are such that they make it possible to use one area (such as technical collaboration) to achieve effects in some other area (such as volumes or trust). In other words, there is a wide variety of possibilities for 'networking' in terms of both means and ends (how and who). Even if a given firm has no intention of using these means actively, it is important to understand them. This is the case both because others in the same network will be using them, and because, irrespective of intentions, all activities have indirect effects. The occurrence and significance of these indirect effects are the first unique feature of networks we discuss.

The second unique feature is closely related to the first – that a large part of any firm's behaviour must be seen as reactions to the behaviour of others. Every measure in a network is related to previous events and future expectations. Even if a person implementing a measure does not intend it as a reaction, it may very well be interpreted as such by other members of the network. When behaviour is seen as a reaction, it is always perceived as directed – in the sense that it works to the benefit of one party and the disadvantage of another. In other words, in addition to having a content, behaviour also has a direction and an impact.

We have already mentioned the third important attribute in the chapter on relationships – the concurrent existence of conflict and co-operation. Any given actor may be one's opponent in some contexts and may perfectly well be a good partner in others. One example of this may be that there is a conflict between a certain part of the purchasing firm and a certain part of the selling firm, at the same time as two other parts of the firms are working closely together. A given partner may also be both one's customer and one's supplier and competitor. In other words, networks interrelate a number of actors, and their relationships are marked both by their contradictory nature and their interaction. For this reason, it is important that a firm's supplier network takes account both of the relationship between the purchasing firm and its individual suppliers as well as the relationships amongst suppliers and between suppliers and other important actors (customers, consultants, etc.).

A fourth major attribute is related to developments within networks. Networks are never entirely stable or in balance. Instead, there are a number of parallel development trends, and one or more of these tend to successively gain strength, while others are weakened. 'Timing' then becomes an extremely important aspect of all action. Working actively with timing means both pushing and being patient. Sometimes time has to be allowed to pass to allow others to adapt, while in other situations there may only be brief openings which must be taken advantage of, since opportunity knocks but once.

All four of the attributes discussed above – the significance of indirect effects, activities which must, at least to some extent, be seen as reactions, the simultaneous occurrence of conflict and collaboration, and the need for timing – are vital characteristics of all networks. A deeper analysis of networks is required to understand their origins and effects, and we make this analysis by using a model of industrial networks developed during the 1980s (Hägg and Johanson 1982, Håkansson and Johanson, 1985, Håkansson 1987 and 1989).

A NETWORK MODEL

To describe and analyse developments in an industrial network, we use a model with three components:

- actors
- activities
- resources

Theoretically, an industrial network consists of actors, interrelated by the fact that they perform complementary or competitive industrial activities resulting in value being added to resources through the consumption of other resources. Each of the three components listed above is dependent on both the others. Actors are characterized by the fact that they perform activities and control resources. Activities are carried out by actors, consuming

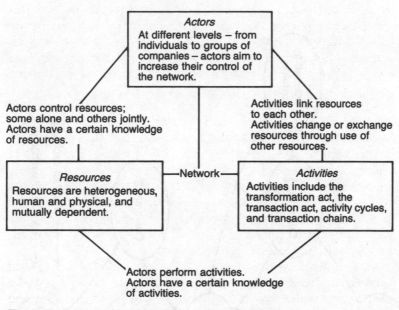

Figure 5.1 Network model (Håkansson 1987: 17)

resources in the process, with a view to adding value to other resources. Ultimately, resources are controlled by actors, and their value is determined by the activities in which they are used. Figure 5.1 indicates some of the main couplings among the three components.

To concretize the model, we begin with a highly simplified supplier network, based on a mechanical engineering firm manufacturing a certain type of equipment. In order to do so, the firm purchases components, one of which is particularly critical to the functioning of the equipment. The firm also purchases some materials and MRO supplies. Last but not least, the firm also buys some production equipment. Figure 5.2 illustrates the most relevant actors in this network.

Even this highly schematic overview of networks provides several examples of dependency amongst the different actors and their activities and resources. When the firm wishes to impact on a relationship, it may take advantage of these dependencies. For instance, to find new solutions to better satisfy its customers, the firms should activate its suppliers as much as possible. It may even be able to affect its suppliers' subcontractors. Alternately, there

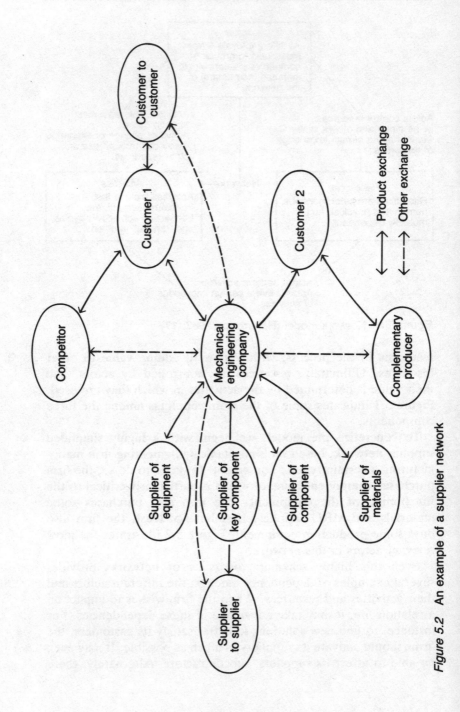

Figure 5.2 An example of a supplier network

Product exchange

Other exchange

may be good reason to co-operate with the complementary producer. Or, seen from the other direction, if the firm wishes to increase the effectiveness of its relationship with a given supplier, the firm may have to convince its customers to make some adaptations with regard either to the technical design of a product, to volumes, or in relation to time. Similarly, an agreement with a competitor as to some standardization of the end product may make it possible to produce larger series which, in turn, may lead to benefits in terms of the effectiveness of supplier relations. Moreover, a change in one supplier relation may enable improvement of another.

This figure shows the diversity of possibilities for affecting/ changing one relationship by acting in relation to another. Irrespective of which relationship we examine, it will always be possible to find examples of ways in which it can be indirectly affected. Combining Figures 5.2 and 5.1, we see how changes in activities may enable exploitation of different resources or vice versa, i.e. how the use of new resources can make it possible to change activities. Let us go on to examine each of the three components – activities, resources and actors, from the buyer's viewpoint.

ACTIVITY ANALYSIS

Looking at existing activities provides a starting point for the analysis of networks. A large number of activities, which must be co-ordinated and integrated, are carried out (both by each of the actors individually and amongst them) at a number of different places. The activities to be performed by suppliers are related to the internal work of the purchasing firm. At the same time, these activities have to be co-ordinated with one another and with what has to be done by the customers and by the different complementary producers. Moreover, they also have to be co-ordinated with activities performed by the suppliers' subcontractors and the customers' customers.

Any given activity is part of various chains of activities. The total cost for performing all activities depends both on how each activity is done, and on how well inter-related these various activities are. Analysis of the production chain often makes it possible to find opportunities for increased effectiveness. This is because the various activities are interconnected, and changing one aspect has effects on others. In other words, for one activity to be simplified or done away with, the activities prior or subsequent to it in the chain must also be changed.

This discussion may be illustrated with an example. If the customers of one firm demand JIT deliveries, the selling firm will have to make in-house changes with relation to its own deliveries, inventories and production and, as a rule, the suppliers to the selling firm will also have to change. In Chapter 3 we described an example from the US of what can happen if a firm tries to isolate JIT to single relationships. The effects are often more negative than positive.

In principle, activities can be made more effective in two ways: first, through replacing individual activities or sets of links in the chain with others, and second through gradual improvement of established chains of activities. The first type of change is analysed below in the section on resource analysis, and the second in the present section. Successive improvements can be made both in terms of the performance of each respective activity and of how the different activities are inter-linked. Here we find an interesting contradiction in terms. The most common means of reducing the cost of an individual activity is through standardization and mass production. However, to bring down the costs related to inter-linked activities requires adaptation, i.e. the opposite of standardization. In recent years, developments in technology and information science have made it possible to take better advantage of the potential for linkage, whereas in the past increasing the effectiveness of individual activities was the most profitable way to make rationalization gains. The remaining problem is that these two means of increasing effectiveness are often at odds with one another.

Within a firm, the two alternatives are often promoted by different categories of personnel which has, at least in some cases, led to a reinforcement of the conflict. Production personnel generally try to cut costs through standardization and mass production, while marketing personnel recommend different forms of customer adaptation, as they are the ones who face the customers' demands. Purchasing managers have a more mixed attitude. Some have worked mostly with standardization in order to make it possible to buy from different suppliers and take advantages of mass production, while others, by working more closely with a smaller number of suppliers, have tried to find better-adapted solutions. The need to achieve a balance between making each individual activity more effective and improving the links between activities will always be with us. Today, the pendulum appears to be about to swing in the direction of thinking that greater profits can be made by improving the linking of activities. The technical development of production equipment and potential communication improvements have opened new opportunities for approaching suppliers and customers and offering them better-adapted solutions. Another contributing factor is the increasing degree of specialization. This has meant that the need for integration between individual units and others which manufacture supplementary products and/or use the end product or service has increased. Firms, and possibly even more so individual production units, have specialized in such limited activities that they cannot possibly stand on their own, without being related to other units. We do not mean to say that specialization has gone too far, or that the trend is turning. On the contrary, all the signs point towards increased specialization. We would simply emphasize that this increases the need for co-ordination and integration with adjacent activities.

To make an activity analysis from a purchasing point of view, a systematic survey is first needed, especially a description of the chains of activities in relation to suppliers and subcontractors. This, however, is not enough. Activity chains, in relation to customers and their customers, must also be included, as well as a survey of the characteristics of the main activities carried out between any of the parties mentioned and any third party (competitor, complementary producer, etc.). Figure 5.2 provides a good point of departure for producing this type of description, and the overview gained from such a survey gives the knowledge needed to address four major issues.

The first is whether to eliminate or relocate some activities by adapting others. Incoming-product control has, for example, been eliminated at some firms by having suppliers guarantee to apply certain quality-control procedures. Many mechanical engineering firms have increased the effectiveness of their assembly activities through integration with suppliers' internal activities, thus reducing their total costs. There are also examples of activities which have been moved backwards from customers to suppliers and vice versa.

The second issue has to do with co-ordination of activities. Can unnecessary costs be eliminated through improved co-ordination? One common example from recent years is inventory costs. For JIT deliveries to be successful, a firm must manage to co-ordinate production activities to such an extent that stocks of input goods and products can be reduced. We have already pointed out the significance of timing, and clearly many kinds of time dependence amongst activities should be taken into account. One of the main ones is time dependence amongst activities in a relationship. Many firms have made great progress in this area, and have often succeeded in co-ordinating quite well with relationships where large volumes are involved. Another kind of time dependence is that between what goes on in a relationship and what goes on in-house for both the buyer and the seller, particularly in terms of dealing with disturbances or change. At the least large firms are trying to build specific demands for flexibility into well-developed relationships. This would give firms the possibility of ordering somewhat smaller or larger volumes, within a given interval, over certain periods of time.

A third type of time dependence is among relationships. For instance, if a purchaser can adapt to the time preferences of some of the seller's other customers, this may lead to a fall in the seller's costs, thanks to mass production or utilization of freed capacity and this, in turn, may lead to price reductions for the buyer. Alternately, the seller may give rise to added value for the buyer, for which the latter is prepared to pay, by adapting to the specific demands of that buyer.

Finally, there is a time dependence between what goes on in the relationship and what goes on in the more general network. For example, before a new product can be accepted it is often necessary for the rest of the network to have adapted to the new technical solution. All four of these time dependencies are important to keep in mind in terms of co-ordination.

Having discussed elimination and/or relocation and co-ordination of activities, we can go on to examine the third issue – adaptation of individual activities in order to make others more effective. Examples include technical adaptations of the supplier's product so that it can be used directly in that of the buyer, or so that it will work better with a product from another supplier. Alternatively, the supplier could provide more exact information in the invoice to facilitate the buyer's incoming-invoice routines, or the buyer might introduce a new order routine to facilitate the production or delivery activities of the supplier. Another example is changes in contacts or working routines in order to improve interaction between two parties. On the whole, there are virtually infinite kinds of adaptations that improve activities and functions.

The fourth and final overall issue is whether any activity or activity chain can be replaced with a different one. For instance, a firm in one area may change technologies (say from mechanical to electronic technology) or materials (say from steel to aluminium or plastic). This kind of change requires supplementing of the resource structure, which is addressed in the next section.

If the purchasing function carries out a systematic review of these four issues, it will usually find that there is a long list of possible measures to implement to improve the activity structure. One of the main results is almost always that the staff realizes the impact their own firm's actions have on the way their suppliers work. If a buyer demands or accepts a particular service, for instance, a form of transport, it contributes to locking the supplier into a certain activity structure. This will always imply costs, which any major purchaser has to pay for. This makes it in the interest of the buyer to encourage suppliers to find the solutions which, totally speaking, are the most effective for them.

RESOURCE ANALYSIS

No activities can be carried out without resources, and activities also generally lead to value being added to resources. This means that how resources are utilized and handled is a major aspect of networking. A firm may acquire advantages by controlling an important resource of limited supply or by utilizing that resource better than other firms. Companies dependent on raw materials have traditionally tried to gain control of the raw-materials source (the mine, the forest, the oil springs, etc.) In previous studies (e.g. Axelsson and Håkansson 1979), we identified five different kinds of resources:

- technical resources (including patents and licences)
- input goods
- personnel
- marketing resources
- capital

The first two of these are particularly important in purchasing contexts, but they are all worth considering.

In the past, different natural resources were the most important input goods. Early mill and foundry industries fought for control of the forests, and the supplies of iron ore and hydro-electric power. These battles were often fierce ones, in which no trick was too dirty. Parties who failed in this had to find technical methods that would make this lack of control less important. For example, in the steel industry, new technologies made it less important to have control of charcoal (the forests) and high-grade iron ore. Since the dawning of the industrial age, control of natural resources has been an important competitive factor, and for many firms it remains so. In the building and construction field, control of gravel and sand pits and land to build on are still vital. However, in recent years other products of an input nature have gained more importance. In the electronics industry, availability of state-of-the-art components may be decisive, as may some substances in biotechnology. This implies that, for input goods, their technology content has gained importance. As we have already pointed out, the importance of suppliers in technical development work has gradually grown. Irrespective of whether what the supplier controls is a natural resource, a specific factory, or an area of knowledge, the control may be an important resource to be utilized in various ways by the purchasing firm. This gives rise to a number of interesting issues.

One of the primary ones is the structure, in principle, of the firm's supplier network, which accounts for a great deal of the external resources of the firm. The current structure must first be surveyed, after which it is possible to discuss how it should be changed in the foreseeable future. This discussion should include at least the following topics:

• What role are external resources to play for the firm? How are suppliers to be utilized in development and rationalization work? Generally, how are they to be combined with the internal resources of the firm? Which resources are so vital that they must always be internally available?
• What fields of knowledge are to be given priority and how is the internal–external distribution to be handled in this respect?
• What processed materials or raw materials are, or may become, central? Who has or may be expected to gain control of them?
• Which fields of technology must the firm keep an eye on or participate in? Who are the central actors in them, and what is the firm's relationship with them?

The next main issue is individual suppliers. Here, too, a survey of which suppliers are crucial at the moment and how the firm utilizes them must be made. In other words, what are the firm's relationships with these suppliers like? Do the suppliers have knowledge or production potential which is not being completely utilized by the buyer? Similarly, an analysis should be made to determine whether there are dimensions in the products and services of the supplier that can be better utilized by the buyer. This type of analysis generally produces many proposals for improvements.

The third issue is combination of resources. There are always a number of untried combinations. Materials may be combined in new ways, as may technical solutions and established knowledge areas. Resource combinations may evolve between the internal resources of the firm and the resources of individual suppliers, amongst various suppliers, and between the resources of suppliers and those of other external units (such as customers). It is never possible to achieve a complete overall picture of all the options, but some common sense and intuition may be helpful.

A fourth issue is the structure of resource control and utilization. Ownership is direct control, but there may be many interesting indirect types as well. In the previous chapter, we discussed relationships as one mechanism of control. A relationship is also a means of utilizing resources. There are a number of intermediate forms such as joint ventures, formal alliances, licensing and co-operation agreements along a spectrum stretching from ownership to informal relations. This makes many forms possible, and their suitability will vary depending on the situation. Moreover, as situations change with time, there is good reason to conduct regular reviews of these structures.

The fifth and final issue is alternative resources. For instance, are there new technical solutions or materials which may be interesting as replacements for current ones? Can the firm test these by approaching new suppliers?

This last item indicates that the activity analysis described in the previous section needs to be linked to the resource analysis. As a rule, activities have to be changed to liberate resources, in the same way that new resources might be necessary to change the activity structure. In the complex industrial reality which comprises the environment of all companies, combinations of resources and activities are undergoing constant change. Change is achieved through interplay amongst the actors involved, and the purchasing firm must always actively participate in this interaction.

ACTOR ANALYSIS

An activity and resource analysis gives a picture of how the company performs, and ensures that this performance is related to the activities and resources of others. An actor analysis is supplementary, in that it focuses on who performs the activities and controls the resources, and how these interrelate. Of course, suppliers are the most important group of actors from a purchasing point of view, but there are also others who impact on how the firm does its purchasing, such as various authorities and organizations who set technical standards. There may also be other large buyers – sometime competitors of the purchasing firm – who actively affect suppliers. Other groups include consultants, technical advisors, and the buying firm's main customers.

Identification of the main actors and how they interrelate is the first step in the actor analysis. The next is to review the attributes of these actors including size, geographical proximity, level of competence, financial strength, and interest in co-operation, with a view to compiling the information necessary to discuss the structure in terms of strengths and weaknesses. Does it need supplementing and/or any major changes? For instance, are there too few suppliers locally? Are there too many actors with limited technical resources, or with financial problems? It may also be important to consider the desire of the actors to co-operate with one's own firm. Examining the structure of the actors indicates areas in which measures can be taken.

One of the first is establishing priorities *vis-à-vis* different counterparts. Who is of primary interest, and in what ways? Such priorities, and limitations, are necessary as it is absolutely impossible to work closely with a large number of suppliers. This is inevitable, despite the fact that it may have negative effects on other (potential) parties. However, it is probably not advisable to make establishing priorities into a formal process. Just because the purpose is to ensure that at least a minimum effort is to be exercised in relation to the selected actors, this must not prevent efforts being made in relation to other actors as well. Priorities are decisions made at a given moment in time, and should not become stereotyped rules to be followed. In other words, priorities are a necessity, but must be subject to constant reappraisal and not taken for granted.

Potential co-ordination is another area in which measures can be taken. Such measures are decided on the basis of the connections between different actors, seeing one's suppliers not only as separate units but also as possible sources of co-ordination. Strategic alliances are often discussed as an important marketing tool, but may be equally important in relation to input goods, for instance when there is limited supply of something, when volume is important owing to economies of scale or other mass-production savings, or where the area of application is limited or expensive.

All in all, there is great potential for co-ordination with regard to actors, their activities and resources. When a purchasing firm is considering what to put first and which parties to co-ordinate with, it must always do so on the basis of its own position or identity. Let us look more closely at how this can be described and analysed.

IDENTITY AND POSITION

To characterize a firm's identity or position in an industrial network, the activity, resource and actor analyses must be combined. Identity and position give a total assessment of how the firm relates to its surrounding units, how its activities are intertwined, how its resources are related, and how the various parties see one another. The terms 'position' and 'identity' are used complementarily here. When one purchasing firm is compared with others, position is used, and the comparison focuses on one or two isolated dimensions. The term 'identity' is used in an effort to combine the diversity of dimensions characterizing the relationship between the individual unit and the surrounding network (the network of which it is a part).

In analysing a firm's position in the field of purchasing, the choice of dimensions is central. Key dimensions may include size (volume), technical specifications or technical attractiveness, and supplier demands. For instance, the firm may be the largest buyer in the country, have average technical specifications, but extremely high delivery demands. This type of positioning provides the information for a discussion of what should characterize a matching partner, how the firm itself should develop to become a more attractive buyer, or how specific partners should be influenced. In other words, positioning always involves comparison.

Identity, on the other hand, should be used to provide a picture of the interplay between the dimensions. For this reason, a firm's identity is always multifaceted, and also always has unique attributes. This means that identity is also relative, but that comparison with others is made on the basis of a whole. This makes it impossible, and perhaps even hazardous, to try to define identity too precisely. Using simple terms is desirable, and the activity, resource and actor analysis described above provides an excellent point of departure. A suitable preliminary sketch might be: 'The specific expertise of the firm is in combining resources x and y with activities z and w in collaboration with actors A, B and C.'

When the identity of a firm is to be analysed, the analysis cannot be limited to purchasing problems. Instead, customers and other external partners (if any) vital to the operations of the firm must be included. There are always a number of potential new combinations. The point of discussing identity is to discover new potential for development. Theoretically, this potential is unlimited. Professor H. Perlmutter, a prominent lecturer on strategy, gave an interesting example at a seminar when he described one exercise he always assigns at his courses for management personnel. He sits them down randomly two by two and tells them to find a means of collaborating – to combine their resources in a new way. Every time but one, this exercise has been successful. The exception was a pair of executives, one from SKF, the other from Nestlé, who proposed 'chocolate-covered ball bearings'.

Professor Perlmutter's findings are at once surprising and completely logical. Firms work in complex ways, and it is natural that two companies can almost always find something to collaborate on, something to combine.

In summary, position and identity are useful terms in combining activities, resources and actors with one another. Position is primarily useful when one or two dimensions are in focus, while identity is a tool for discussing how the firm as a whole relates to its network.

NETWORK ANALYSIS – IN SUMMARY

This chapter had a clear and simple message: all activities, resources and actors are interconnected or interdependent, and this can be used to advantage, because the connections give every network a unique reaction pattern. To understand what happens, to be able to analyse an isolated measure correctly, it is necessary to be aware of this reaction pattern. It determines the rules of the game, and the ability of individual actors to affect things. It is also important to keep in mind that this pattern is not stable, but constantly in flux.

This chapter also contains proposals for working methods to understand better what happens in networks. Describing and analysing the separate structures applying to activities, resources and actors, and then combining them in terms of positions and identities make it possible to capture some of their main attributes. The following is a summary of our network analysis of purchasing issues in the form of a first outline of a checklist. However, it should be considered a first attempt, and furthermore it is never possible to identify everything, as the process itself gives rise to insights as to new possibilities and activities, and these in turn change the network. This means that the aim of each analysis is simply to propose measures, and not to determine a certain stereotyped behaviour, once and for all.

Activity analysis

Survey and analysis of all the chains of activities of which the firm's own activities are a part

1 What does a complete activity chain from subcontractor to the customer's customer look like?
2 Can any activity be eliminated or moved to another actor's sphere?
3 Can co-ordination of activities be improved?
4 Can any activity be made more effective by adapting it better to other activities?
5 Can any given activity chain be replaced by any other?

Resource analysis

Survey and analysis of the firm's resource situation in the total network

1 What are the critical factors for the firm in the five resource dimensions (input goods, technology, personnel, capital, marketing)?

2 Which of these critical resources must be controlled by the firm, and which can be procured externally?
3 Which other actors control these critical resources today?
4 What are our current relations to these suppliers? What forms for co-operation can we establish to gain access to their resources?
5 Can our current suppliers be encouraged to change in a way that will give us as buyers access to a more extensive repertoire of resources?

Actor analysis

Survey and analysis of the main actors in the network and the relationships among them

1 What characterizes the central actors – size, competence, location, financial strength?
2 What are the attributes of our own supplier structure in relation to these factors? State strengths and weaknesses.
3 What changes need to be made and what needs to be supplemented with regard to relations with other actors in light of item 2 above and in relation to our own activity and resource analyses?
4 Which counterparts should be given priority in order to establish a good future structure? How should our priorities be determined?
5 What measures can we take to co-ordinate in order to better utilize other actors? This may include collaboration with suppliers, other buyers, etc.

Chapter 6

Purchasing developments – five cases

In Chapters 4 and 5, we analysed relationships and networks from a purchasing point of view. A number of important dimensions and issues were identified and discussed, and managerial implications drawn. We also presented some small examples and illustrations, despite the impossibility of giving a complete picture. In the present chapter, five more extensive case studies are presented. Our choice of cases has been directed by several aims. First, and most importantly, the intention is to illustrate different types of purchasing situations. Thus, our purpose is to present both problems regarding purchasing of specific types of products as well as the total purchasing strategy of a firm. Second, we want to give examples from very different technological and geographical environments, in order to show that the same types of analyses are relevant in most situations. One type of situation – procurement of automotive components – was excluded, owing to its overrepresentation in other purchasing literature, and to the fact that it was well covered in our discussion in Chapter 3. But we do include one case from an automotive industry – Volvo – dealing with procurement of MRO supplies.

PROCUREMENT OF MRO SUPPLIES FOR A CONSTRUCTION COMPANY

The first case has been chosen as it provides a wonderful example of what can be accomplished when a buying and a selling company start to discuss common issues more openly. Even for very mundane products, there are major advantages to be gained in linking the activities of the companies together and finding new ways of doing business that has already been going on for a long time. However, some very important conditions must be established. One is that both sides have a long-term perspective – this case study covers more than six years. Another is that both sides must have a clear ambition to develop their relationship, and be able to agree to work together in some important key dimensions to improve it. Another prerequisite is that the achievements must be continuously followed up.

The companies involved

This case study deals with a long-term project aiming at developing a new way of handling the procurement of MRO supplies. The customer is a division of a construction company in Sweden. The name of the buying division is Huse and it is part of SIAB, the third largest construction company in Sweden. Huse's annual turnover is approximately Sw.Kr. 300 million. The division in question is concentrated to one region in Sweden.

Procurement of materials and tendering for subcontracts are handled by two purchasers who divide their work geographically. Huse has a central warehouse at the head office, from which equipment and machinery, etc., are rented out to the different projects (sites). Previously, the central warehouse had a larger sphere of responsibility and did most of the purchasing for the projects.

The seller is the Österberg company, a distributor of hardware products. Österberg is part of Järnia, the major chain in the hardware-supplies business in Sweden. They sell their products partly through their own sales shop in Karlstad, and partly through a distribution system in which Österberg delivers, with its own fleet of lorries to its customers' sites or factories. The distribution system accounts for most of their sales.

The company has a total of 30 employees, some of whom run the shop, while others specialize in taking telephone orders and expediting deliveries.

A development project

The first contacts were initiated in March, 1984. Erik Asplund (purchasing director of SIAB) and Urban Dane (marketing director of Järnia) were in touch for other reasons, but started to talk about the possibility of having a joint project around the distribution of hardware supplies. Asplund began discussions at Huse and Dane at Österberg. These two units were chosen because they were perceived as being positively oriented towards development and having had good relations in the past. The precise aim of the project was formulated by Huse and Österberg as creating a rational flow of supplies to the different Huse sites. At that time Huse used many different suppliers and had very little control either of what products were bought or of how the buying was done. In order to get a first overview, it was decided that a new specific catalogue should be produced, in which Huse and Österberg, in co-operation, would specify the product mix. The content of the catalogue was successively identified at a sequence of meetings. Ultimately, it consisted of about 4,000 items, in contrast with the 120,000-item standard catalogue that was previously used.

During the same time period (late 1984 and early 1985) the personnel in the two companies were informed of the plans. Two special meetings were held where the personnel from each side met for discussions.

A first draft of the catalogue was finished in April 1985, and was discussed by both companies. The final version was distributed to all nineteen sites in June, 1985. On 19 June Lennart Svensson, purchasing manager at Huse, issued a letter to all site managers saying 'Okay, let's go ahead!'

On 31 October 1985 all of the relevant Huse managers were invited to Österberg, which had moved into new offices. Once again information was given about the company, the catalogue, the distribution system and the product suppliers.

The effects of the project

The relationship between the two parties has developed very nicely, as is shown in Table 6.1. However, this development has only been achieved through highly intense and very conscious ambition on both sides. Again and again, revitalizing activities have been undertaken. Most of these have taken place when some of the variables that were chosen for systematic follow-up were showing negative trends. There is thus good reason to identify and measure the development of some of these key variables. One main cause of occasional problems has been the activities of other suppliers, who have reacted in different ways.

Table 6.1 Österberg's importance as Huse's supplier

Year	Volume per month	Share of Huse's purchased volume of the product group
	Sw.Kr.	
1983	42000	Approximately 16%
1984	61000	
1985	120000	
1986	120000	
1987	160000	
1988	200000	
1989	260000	Approximately 65%

One of the ambitions of the project was to concentrate procurement on one supplier – Österberg – and development in this respect can be seen in Table 6.1.

Huse has also become a more important customer to Österberg. In 1985, Huse accounted for approximately 4 per cent of Österberg's sales, and this share has successively increased. Huse has thus managed to gain control over the procurement of supplies. Today, Österberg provides Huse with data showing the consumption of various products at each site. The variation in the product mix has been limited. This has also had positive effects for Österberg, which has increased its volumes of certain products and thus also its opportunities for handling them cost-effectively.

The material flow follows two different paths from Österberg to Huse. One is when Huse employees purchase products directly from Österberg. This means that they leave their sites, go to the Österberg shop, buy the product there and return to the site with it. Taking the other path, they order by telephone and have the products delivered through the Österberg distribution system (lorries that follow certain routes in accordance with a set timetable). One of the ambitions of the project was to increase utilization of this second path. Initially, this was perceived by the Huse representatives as impossible, as the site managers claimed that their needs could not be planned. Developments are shown in Table 6.2.

We can see from the table that it has become possible to plan procurement to a much higher extent than any of the site managers believed at the start. The material flow now follows a much more highly planned, and thus a much more cost-effective route.

Another ambition was to lower administrative costs. One of the

Table 6.2 Use of the Österberg distribution system

Year	Through store	Through Österberg's distribution system
	%	%
1984	95	5
1985	74	26
1986	52	48
1987	35	65
1988	22	78
1989	19	81

Table 6.3 Number of invoices per month and their average amounts (measured during one month)

Year	Number	Average amount
		Sw.Kr.
1984	75	812
1985	71	1,608
1986	58	2,129
1987	33	5,000
1988	60	3,312
1989	43	5,912

dimensions chosen for measurement was the number of invoices and their average amounts. The goal was to decrease the number of invoices by increasing their average amounts. Developments can be seen in Table 6.3.

In analysing Table 6.3, it is important to remember how the total volume has increased, which means that the intended effects were successful every year with the exception of 1988. The results from that year initiated a revitalization of the relationship during 1989.

Economic consequences for Huse

During the early phase of the development process, a study was carried out with regard to the way Huse organized their procurement activities. In that study, the site managers were asked to calculate the number of trips made from their site to Österberg's or other distributors for purchases in stores. At the same time the distances and the time for the trips were calculated. This study was conducted in 1985, when Huse used the Österberg distribution system for 26 per cent of their deliveries (see Table 6.2). At that time, Huse personnel (from all sites) drove some 11,000 km per month to buy products, and spent a total of 275 hours doing so. Data from the companies, published in Asplund and Wootz (1986), shows that the total cost for this way of handling the material flow was calculated to be Sw.Kr. 87,000 per month in 1984. From Table 6.1 we know that in the same year the price paid for the goods purchased was Sw.Kr. 61,000 per month. This provides a good illustration of the substantial magnitude of indirect costs when purchasing MRO supplies. The savings obtained in 1985, when an increasing proportion of the purchased volume was delivered through Österberg's distribution system, were considerable. When the portion of purchases from Österberg's shop decreased from 95 per cent to 74 per cent (Table 6.2), the savings were calculated to be Sw.Kr. 22,000 per month. Given the same rationale, the savings by 1989 can be estimated to have been another Sw.Kr. 48,000 per month.

All these calculations are specific to these firms and cannot be applied to other companies, but they do show how significant handling costs are for this product type, and what can be done in terms of collaborating more closely with one counterpart.

Case comments

One reason we chose to begin with this case is that it is such a good illustration of our discussion in Chapter 4, and a perfect example of what can be accomplished when a 'loose' relationship is developed into a more solid one. The need for a long-term perspective is obvious, as is the need for building up reciprocal trust. The adaptations made on each side are the key mechanisms in developing the relationship and the two parties become interdependent. This increasing dependency tends to increase the tension in the relationship. Owing to the existence of trust, however, this tension can generally be put to fruitful use. Thus, each of the sections in Chapter 4 is illustrated by the case study. It is interesting to note that it would be cheaper for Österberg if the Huse personnel came to the store for their purchases. The total costs for the relationship, however, can be substantially decreased by use of Österberg's more advanced delivery system. Although Österberg's costs increase when this system is used, they are compensated through the increased volume and a more focused demand, which enables it to decrease its costs in a different way.

It is also possible to analyse the case using the kind of network analysis proposed in Chapter 5. The two companies decided to relate their activities and resources in a tighter way after an actor analysis had been conducted. Huse decided to give Österberg more priority. Earlier Österberg was seen as one supplier among several others. Now it was given first priority. Österberg had developed a certain distribution system in collaboration with industrial producers and it wanted to use the same system in relation to construction companies. As Huse showed an interest, they became the pilot case. Over the years the two companies improved the linking of their activities, and this made their resources more complementary. The project has also affected their identities in the networks. Both companies use the project not only to expand this relationship, but on others as well. There have been a number of attempts from other companies to prevent the increasing co-operation between Österberg and Huse. Other suppliers of the same products have tried to protect their relationships with Huse and it took Huse a long time to break off these relationships. Some of them survived, and have gone on developing. This may be of great interest in the long run for Huse.

This first case study dealt with the development of one relationship. In the next one, we present an example where the purchasing firm tries to develop a whole chain of supplier relationships.

PROCUREMENT OF MRO SUPPLIES FOR VOLVO

The second case study deals with the same type of products as the first – mundane, everyday supplies – but in relation to another type of buyer technology. The customer is Volvo. The type of large-scale, mass production that characterizes the automotive industry made car companies aware from an early stage of the need to link their activities with those of their suppliers. In order to achieve more substantial rationalization benefits, they have to extend their analysis and involvement several steps backward into the supplier network.

The 'change project'

Roos (1988) reports on a change project carried out at Volvo, the aim of which was to make operations more effective by closer co-operation with suppliers. The project was carried out at the procurement and purchasing department of the Volvo Car Corporation between 1984 and 1987. In emulation of the Japanese experience, efforts were being made to increase delivery frequency and decrease lot sizes purchased. To achieve this, a number of substantial changes were required. One was that purchasing decisions of a routine nature were taken directly by the operational units. In these cases, they made their requisitions directly to the supplier, via computerized communication, instead of via the purchasing department, as had previously been the case. This made it possible to decrease lead times from two weeks to twenty-four hours. A new purchasing strategy was also adapted. The previous strategy had been to have at least two suppliers of each individual product. In order to work with JIT deliveries and total quality control, the intended modification was to purchase all that was needed of a given product group from a single supplier, which was meant to lead to a tangible reduction in the number of suppliers. However, it proved to be difficult to reduce the number of suppliers in this way. Many articles had unique properties and were not interchangeable. Therefore, the new principle gradually became that of asking one firm to supply the entire volume of a given article. In a few cases it became possible to further reduce

Table 6.4 Effects of changes in purchasing behaviour

	Warehouse		
	1	2	3
Purchased volume (index)			
Before	100	100	100
After	137	151	133
Number of articles (index)			
Before	100	100	100
After	100	540	81
Inventory volume (index)			
Before	100	100	100
After	65	30	44
Delivery times (days)			
Before		21	12
After		2	5
Delivery reliability (no. of back orders/time unit)			
Before		1500	1800
After		100	160

the number of suppliers by having others increase their product range.

Effects at Volvo

Three inventory units were affected by this project for change: tools and MRO supplies, uniforms and work boots. The change project went on for three years, with the following effects (see Table 6.4).

Stock reduction was particularly notable in warehouses 2 and 3, where it was cut back by substantially more than half, despite volume increases of 33 to 51 per cent. The number of articles kept in stock remained unchanged in one case, but increased considerably in warehouse 2 and decreased slightly in warehouse 3.

It was also found that the stock reduction could be combined with improvements in service level. There are no statistics from warehouse 1, but both the others indicate shortened delivery times and increased delivery reliability (a sharp decrease in the number of back orders).

Thus it can be seen that it was possible for the Volvo warehouses to increase their degree of service in spite of substantial reductions of the goods in stock, with a consequent reduction in capital costs. It is interesting to find that even greater savings could be made in relation to other costs in materials administration. The primary effects here were a result of its becoming possible to eliminate one warehouse, which meant a need for fewer facilities, less administration and handling, and shorter process times. Another considerable rationalization benefit was that, once the goods reception centre was moved, less quality-control work was necessary, and previous repetition of work was eliminated. The total effect of these cost reductions was nearly twice as great as the reduction of capital costs *per se*.

In the process of obtaining these effects, other costs increased. Improvement of in-house handling necessitated renovation of a warehouse, and investment in equipment for effective, flexible stock handling. The warehouses were also brightened up to increase personnel satisfaction and motivation.

The estimates made of the total effect indicated that these changes resulted in annual savings corresponding to 25 per cent of the tied-up capital of the warehouse.

Effects on the suppliers

Roos also describes how the suppliers were involved in this process of change. One of his examples relates to deliveries of uniforms. The supplier (Tvättman) is situated in the immediate vicinity of Gothenburg, and supplies Volvo with new uniforms as well as laundering the ones already in use. This amounts to 85,000 articles per year, of which one-third are replaced annually. This clothing is manufactured by the Bergis company, which has three plants in western Sweden, which deliver 55 per cent of their production to Tvättman. One of Bergis' most important suppliers is an Italian cloth manufacturer (Klopman).

Figure 6.1   The supply chain

In the introductory section of this case study we primarily analysed in-house effects at Volvo warehousing, and what happened in relationship A. Let us go on to examine effects on other relationships.

Volvo is one of Tvättman's main customers. For this reason, the changes initiated by Volvo had substantial effects when they were passed along via relationship B. The increased demand thus also meant that Tvättman had to change its purchasing behaviour. First, there had to be in-house changes with regard to its view of customer and supplier relations. Secondly, there had to be changes in actual working methods. To prevent Tvättman's stock from increasing owing to measures implemented at Volvo, it was necessary for Tvättman, in turn, to become more effective with regard to frequency of deliveries and lot sizes in relationship C. Ordering routines were changed so that Tvättman in Gothenburg submitted its orders directly to Bergis via telex. Previously, it had ordered by writing to its own head office in Malmö, which then placed the order with Bergis. This made it possible to shorten the lead time from two weeks to twenty-four hours.

For Tvättman, the effect was that stock volumes decreased by more than one third, despite the fact that the volume of uniforms handled increased by over one third during the three-year period.

Service – in terms of delivery reliability – also improved from 85 to 97.3 per cent, in spite of the substantial increase in the number of items.

Tvättman's demands shifted down to the next link in the chain (Bergis). Bergis has not decreased its total stock of finished garments, because in conjunction with these changes Bergis began to serve as a central warehouse for special garments for all 24 Tvättman plants. The result was that both volume and number of articles increased for Bergis. Relatively, therefore, its stock of the garments it previously supplied has dropped considerably, in part thanks to changes in its work organization.

Production workers previously performed only specialized parts of the process. In principle, this meant that twelve people contributed to every finished garment. Personnel received training to raise their competence, and today only one to three people are needed to sew each whole garment. The effects of this were that the production pipeline was shortened from nine to three weeks, and an estimated productivity improvement of 5 to 10 per cent. To make it possible to live up to the demands of JIT delivery and handling of the increased number of articles, the firm computerized its production, inventory and delivery follow-up and monitoring.

Bergis' orders, in turn (relationship D), also changed in the direction of increased frequency and smaller lots. The result of this has been a 60-per-cent decrease in the stock of cloth on hand, and a drop in lead time from eight to three weeks. The firm itself claims that these changes in suborder routines have had no effect at all on the Italian cloth supplier, in whose total production volume Bergis is a marginal customer.

Case comments

The benefits of analysing the interface between the suppliers and the purchasing company's in-house activities is well illustrated by this case. Volvo is systematically trying to develop its supplier network for MRO supplies. The aim of these activities is not just to decrease costs, but also to improve the service level. The lesson to be learned is that the purchasing company must develop its own planning work and improve its execution of administrative and physical tasks to find out better ways of using its suppliers. Activities must be analysed step by step, through several links of companies, stretching from the buying firm, through the supplier, the subcontractor and eventually even the sub-subcontractor. For other products, such as components, this analysis should also be expanded forward to customers and their customers. This systematic analysis and co-ordination of the activity chain may show substantial potential for rationalization improvements whenever large quantities are handled. So when a company buys large quantities of any product (materials, components or MRO supplies) attempts should always be made to analyse the chain at least a few steps back.

The need to adapt resources to facilitate the close linking of activities can also be found in this case study. Volvo had to invest in order to implement its new way of using its suppliers, and so did the suppliers. This mutual investment process facilitates the interaction, but it also increases the mutual dependence of the counterparts.

The investments made in this case are small compared to what is needed when co-operation concerns the development of new products. Such a project is the theme of the next case study.

BIOPHARM'S USE OF SUPPLIERS IN DEVELOPING A NEW PRODUCT

Our third case study is an illustration of using suppliers in an active way in terms of technical development. The case deals with the development of a new system and the role the suppliers can play in developing different components of that system. The case illustrates the need for an actor analysis, in order to find suppliers who are both willing to be and are capable of being development partners. Other important issues are financial compensation for the suppliers and the need to involve the right personnel in the relationships. The data for this case study have been collected through interviews and from written documents, project documentation, etc. The interviews were made with four members of the project team, including the project leader and the product manager, and with two of the suppliers involved (Eriksson 1989).

Biopharm and its product

Biopharm (disguised name) is a company which designs, manufactures and markets systems for the production of pharmaceuticals. It is a relatively large company, operating on a global basis.

In the early 1980s, Biopharm began manufacturing 'The System'. This system was used for the purification of pharmaceutical raw materials. It was produced in units or small lots, mainly for special orders, and the number produced and sold was about 30 units a year. Customer needs regarding quality and design were different, so the systems were often tailored to the buyer's requirements.

The production of the system was highly specialized, i.e. it was built mainly from components purchased from external suppliers. Purchased components made up about 85 per cent of the total production cost of the system.

Another characteristic of the original system was that only about 20 per cent of its components were technically adapted to the system, while 80 per cent were purely standard. This fact made supplier contacts easy to handle, not least from a technical point of view.

The development project

In 1987, Biopharm decided to update and redesign the system to develop one single version. Biopharm wanted the system to be of high quality, as the buyers with high-quality requirements were growing in number. One important means of enhancing the quality was to obtain components that were well adapted to their functions in this particular system. In the original version, the large proportion of standard components led to a number of technical compromises in the system, or as one technician from Biopharm expressed the problem: 'The system was a mish-mash of more or less well suited components, and badly documented.'

Biopharm assigned a project group to redesign the system. The group started out by determining the functional standards of the system as a whole. Then every part was gone through carefully, and detailed specifications for individual components set. At this stage, some discussions and inquiries were carried out with component suppliers. It was not, however, until the specifications were ready and set, that a more systematic call for tenders was issued.

The companies that already supplied Biopharm with standard components for the original system then received inquiries concerning the new technical specifications. The majority of the old suppliers, however, turned out to be either unable or unwilling to meet the new requirements. Some of them were large companies, and quite uninterested in adapting their standardized products just to satisfy a relatively small customer such as Biopharm. Actually, only two out of the approximately thirty former suppliers of major components (minor details excluded) turned out to be potential suppliers.

In effect, most of the components needed could not be obtained from the existing suppliers. This meant that much of the project work had to be devoted to contacts and discussions with a large number of potential new suppliers. Some 30–40 major components had to be purchased, and throughout the project Biopharm was in touch with various suppliers of each one.

A number of suppliers presented samples and prototypes. An important task for Biopharm was to run tests on these in their own laboratory. These tests required competence within fields of knowledge related to the use of the system. Therefore the tests could not be performed by the component suppliers. This testing was time consuming, and progress in the collaboration with individual suppliers was often delayed, pending test results.

Many of the suppliers under consideration by Biopharm during the project, were either dropped or accepted but backed out after only a few contacts. During the process, however, a core of 12–15 especially interesting partners crystallized. An intensive discussion with these suppliers then evolved. Many people from each side were involved and engaged in frequent contacts, technical discussions, visits, etc. Among these innovative relation-ships, the two remaining old suppliers were found. Not surprisingly, they both had 20–25 year connections with Biopharm, and each of them supplied components that constituted a large proportion of the total system value.

The technical specifications demanded by Biopharm were some-times perceived by the suppliers as being nearly impossible to fulfil. One example was a valve manufacturer who was asked to make a new type of valve, cast in one piece. To begin with, the supplier found the whole idea absurd and rejected the proposition.

Table 6.5 Supplier structure of 'The System'

Total number of suppliers	60
Suppliers of major components	30
Old suppliers of major components	2
New suppliers of major components	28
Suppliers with close collaboration during the project	12–15

However, after a lot of involvement on the part of their own technicians, Biopharm eventually made the supplier see the point of the proposed design. The supplier began to see the idea more as a 'new way of thinking' and decided to give it a try. The new type of valve was not completed by the time of the launching of the new system in the fall 1989, but the first delivery was expected by the end of the year.

Biopharm's persistence – and sometimes 'absurd' requirements – made the company quite a fussy customer to deal with. Nevertheless, their demands and ideas also made them an interesting and stimulating partner. Some of the suppliers perceived their interaction with Biopharm as an opportunity to develop their own field of competence.

Biopharm's relationships with its two former suppliers developed even more during this project, and assumed a somewhat different character. Both suppliers were foreign companies, whose sales to Biopharm had previously been handled entirely through local agents. During this project, however, technical matters became too complex to handle via intermediaries. Therefore a direct dialogue between Biopharm and the manufacturers was established. In other words, the earlier standardized, routine ways of handling these relationships were not adequate when the product was no longer standardized. Both the social and technical exchange between the companies was extended, as was the number of people involved in the relationship.

The financial side of the collaboration was managed in different ways in different relationships. Some of the suppliers were very small firms, not able to finance development costs themselves. Such firms also saw very little possibility of benefiting from the outcome in other areas. In some of these cases Biopharm either paid for the whole or part of the cost and thereby obtained exclusive rights to the product. In other cases, however, the supplier was large enough to bear the expense and also saw possibilities in other areas. Some of these companies were offered financial support by Biopharm, but refused it, since Biopharm required exclusive rights in return.

Not all collaborative attempts in this project were successful. One of the 12–15 promising relationships mentioned earlier was with a domestic manufacturer of electronic instruments. This was a very small company, specialized in a narrow niche. The instrument Biopharm wanted them to design was unique. The supplier seemed receptive to Biopharm's technical instructions, and at the beginning of the collaboration both parties were quite optimistic. The supplier began working on the product, and over the next 4–5 months the firms had frequent contact. The supplier behaved as if everything was working out as planned. When the first delivery arrived, however, the product was not at all satisfactory. Technical discussions continued. The supplier still wanted to proceed with the project. One year later, Biopharm had major doubts about the outcome of this collaboration, and was seriously considering dropping the supplier. It was discovered that the supplier had considerable problems connected with the establishment of a production unit in Southeast Asia. According to Biopharm, the supplier had not been frank about the scope or impact of its internal problems.

In the successful cases of collaboration, i.e. where a satisfactory component was obtained, Biopharm's efforts and active participation in the suppliers' development work seems to have been of great importance. First, especially in the completely new relationships, Biopharm's commitment was necessary to reinforce the suppliers' faith in the project. In this way resources could more easily be mobilized. Second, the input of Biopharm's knowledge about the function of a supplier's component in this particular application was important to the supplier. Third, because Biopharm's expertise was mainly in a different field than that of the suppliers, 'absurd' – but also innovative – solutions were suggested and new ways of thinking could sometimes be found.

Results

When the project was completed, the outcome was a system that fulfilled Biopharm's expectations with regard to quality and design. Proper documentation had also been accomplished. The original version of the system had consisted of 20 per cent specially designed or adapted components and 80 per cent standard components. In the new version these proportions were reversed. These results could to a large extent be considered as products of the close collaboration between Biopharm and the suppliers.

The outcome of the project could, however, be seen in other respects besides the quality of the system developed. First, because of the technical adaptations in the new components and also because of the documentation produced for the components,

Biopharm's new supplier relationships are much tighter than were the old ones. For most of the components there is now only one supplier, which would be rather difficult to replace quickly.

Second, the social bonds with suppliers have become rather strong since a lot of people got to know each other during the development process.

Third, indirect technical dependencies between different suppliers have been created as their components are all adapted to fit the system. In effect, one supplier cannot change his component without affecting the functioning of other components.

Fourth, new ways of thinking and developed knowledge within supplier companies could open new possibilities for them in other networks.

Case comments

It is interesting to compare Biopharm's supplier network for its earlier system with its new one. In producing the first system, Biopharm was in contact with a group of suppliers with no connections between them. The relationships were not especially developed, i.e. Biopharm simply bought products, standardized items, that had been developed for other applications. It was easy for Biopharm to change suppliers, because there were always other suppliers who could offer them the same products. All units were relatively independent.

The new structure moves Biopharm to the other end of the spectrum, with all the relationships, and thus also the companies, much more dependent on one another. The products are much more specialized and they fit together in a much more integrated way than before. There are even dependencies among suppliers. Today, it is quite difficult for Biopharm to change a single supplier. Such a process takes time and means a loss of investments. On the other hand, all the suppliers are under pressure. If the final system becomes too expensive there will be no sales, which will affect them all, independently and as a whole. They could, of course, use extortion upon one another, but only for a short time because there is still the opportunity to exchange any part of the system. If a supplier has to be changed, it will never be given a second chance. The new network thus contains much more tension than the first. As long as this tension can be used constructively, however, it will be beneficial to most of them. But there may always be a loser. If the costs of making the adaptations are larger than the revenues accrued from Biopharm or some other complementary relationships, the supplier will operate at a loss. As is shown in this case study, a number of the previous suppliers decided that this might be the case for them when they chose not to participate.

The necessity of interplay between the competence of the purchasing company and that of its suppliers for development of an effective network is thus brought into focus. This is further elaborated on in the next case, where a purchasing firm works systematically to educate its suppliers in order to make them better partners.

MOTOROLA AND A SUPPLIER–DEVELOPMENT PROGRAMME

Our first two cases dealt with purchasing problems in terms of how to develop individual relationships or how to develop a supplier network for a certain type of purchased products. The third case extended the problems into the development of products and knowledge. In the last two, we extend the analysis one step further and look at the whole company's supplier network. In the first case study we show how Motorola has developed a general training programme in an attempt to develop more or less all of its suppliers. This case provides us with a good illustration of the need to make the long-term purchasing strategy very clear, in order to communicate it effectively to suppliers. Even then, however, complementary activities must be undertaken to stress the importance of this issue.

Supplier involvement

Motorola, Inc. is one of the world's leading manufacturers of electronic-equipment systems and components. During the 1980s, the company has become a well-known example of a promoter of total quality. Our case description is based on Cayer (1988).

Of every Motorola sales dollar, between 30 and 60 per cent (depending on the business group) goes to suppliers. This alone makes it quite clear that suppliers have a heavy impact on the quality of Motorola products. Company representatives think that suppliers 'affect quality more than any other factor in the equation' except for design. Owing to increasing foreign competition, Motorola is committed to accelerating its quality-improvement programme. For this process to be successful, considerable supplier improvement is vital.

Supplier involvement is known to be a major source of potential for improving competitiveness. One company representative states that all the Motorola factories have made tremendous efforts and gains in product quality, reduction of cycle times, and cost reductions. Although some suppliers have played important roles in these improvements, the majority of the supplier base is considered not to have kept up with the pace of Motorola.

Four demands on suppliers that are part of the Motorola improvement process are stated. Motorola needs suppliers who:

• keep pace in attaining perfect quality
• are on the leading edge of technology
• use JIT manufacturing
• offer cost-competitive service.

According to the company, stating the requirements is the easy part – the difficult thing is implementing them. Motorola has worked with supplier development for a number of years. The major problem has been to change the culture associated with the relationships – from the old adversarial type to 'win-win' partnerships. After observing good examples at other companies (such as Rank Xerox and Ford) Motorola has been able to improve supplier relations through a series of programmes carried out with their suppliers.

Training and education of suppliers

Training and education were very important factors in the internal quality programme at Motorola. They estimate that they invested 40 million dollars annually in training in more sophisticated manufacturing, design and management techniques. In the beginning, the programmes were open only to the employees of Motorola. Then, through an analysis of best-practice firms Motorola found that one significant difference between itself and Ford and Rank Xerox was that these companies had extended their training to suppliers as well. Motorola considered that fact to be an important key to its subsequent success.

This was the starting point for the supplier-training programme established in 1988, with the aim of training suppliers to keep up to par in efficiency and productivity. The reason Motorola provided this programme was that its training courses had already been proved to work internally, and it had gained a great deal of hard-earned experience when developing them. Another reason was that only a small part of the supplier base would have had the resources necessary to develop the kind of training needed.

The benefits of the partnership training programmes are mutual. Motorola, of course, has a vested interest in improving supplier performance as they are a part of the assembly line. But suppliers also stand to gain, as the training provided by Motorola will strengthen their overall competitive power. They will be able to broaden their customer base to include other companies striving for zero defects.

The Motorola training programme provides us with an illustration of the structural role of purchasing. By increasing their strength and capabilities, suppliers become more competitive. In the US a trend has developed in that many domestic suppliers have encountered difficulties because foreign competitors are more efficient. According to one Motorola representative, there are several component categories for which there are no longer any domestic suppliers. An increasing dependency on foreign suppliers is not considered a desirable future by Motorola. Therefore it is in its own interest to help develop and promote the capabilities of domestic suppliers so that they will be able to make significant quality improvements.

The programme

Motorola began by establishing a 'partnerships for growth advisory board', which initiated a programme with three courses. These training courses covered SPC (statistical process control), design for manufacturability and short-cycle management (where the JIT concept is introduced).

Suppliers were made aware of the courses in a letter signed by the general managers of the Motorola divisions concerned, with a brochure enclosed describing the Partnership for Growth Training Series. Response was limited and suppliers were encouraged again, and were also reminded of the fact that the completion of the three courses was a condition for ongoing business. Even then reactions were slow in coming. Many suppliers felt they didn't need the training. Others were so established that SPC appeared to them to be a basic technique. After almost one year Motorola increased the pressure on suppliers and insisted that suppliers had to take all three courses if they were interested in doing business in the future. The reason for this increasing pressure was the findings presented in a five-year study conducted by the Automotive Industry Action Group, which indicated that suppliers implemented technology, JIT and other viable programmes only to the extent enforced by their customers, and that they did not take opportunities to improve their own productivity.

Motorola considered this a serious drawback to the future competitiveness of suppliers, and intensified its pressure on them. After five more months, 167 of the 500 suppliers intended for the programme had completed courses. The results achieved were considered very substantial by Motorola representatives. Within some weeks of basic SPC training, suppliers had made dramatic leaps towards better quality.

The supplier-training programme is only one of a number of activities undertaken to encourage partnership in relationships. Another is promotion of early supplier involvement in new product development. In a number of commodity-product areas, the suppliers' technicians are considered to be the true experts. Therefore, a growing interest has been shown in many of the divisions of the company in facilitating participation of supplier technicians in new product development from a very early stage.

The Communication Sector, Motorola's largest business, encourages supplier participation by focusing on four formalized functions – the supplier advisory board, annual conferences, annual technical symposia and the supplier show. The supplier advisory board was formed to improve two-way communication between Motorola and a core of selected suppliers. The annual supplier conferences provide an exchange of information and insights into various business activities. Conference speakers are always top managers at Motorola. This is an indication to the suppliers of the importance the corporation attaches to the conference and to the development of supplier partnerships. The technical symposia and supplier shows provide Motorola's engineering, manufacturing and purchasing people with an awareness of a broad range of products and technologies available from suppliers. The symposia take the form of in-depth technical seminars on topics presented by technical experts from supplier companies.

Case comments

It might appear relatively uncomplicated to change a purchasing strategy. However, doing so requires a complete change in the way relationships with suppliers are handled. Only when there are no previous relationships to have an influence, might it be easy to change one's own strategy, but in all other cases a change has a substantial effect on how the suppliers should work. Making this type of change takes a long time and is extremely demanding on resources, as can be seen in the case of Motorola. Even for such a very large buyer, it proved difficult to get the suppliers to take an active part in development work.

There is some resistance to change in all networks. This makes it necessary to work with systematic mobilization strategies. Nothing will be accomplished without the support of the counterparts, and all changes must, accordingly, be seen from the other actors' point of view. Neither purchasing nor marketing strategies can be formulated only from the point of view of one's own company. For changes to be accepted by other actors, therefore, both purchasing and marketing, must be analysed and structured so as to create business opportunities for other parts of the network as well.

This type of network strategy can be seen in the last case study, of Nike.

NIKE'S NETWORK STRATEGIES FOR SUBCONTRACTING

One of the keys to a successful network strategy for purchasing is making the different suppliers systematically interrelated. One of the aims is to mobilize the suppliers for development and production in what the buying company considers the right way. In this last case study, Nike's purchasing strategy stands as an illustration of how this can be done.

Nike's supplier network

Nike is a major US athletic footwear producer. The case study deals with their supplier network structure and strategy. It is based on information in an article written by Donaghu and Barff (1990).

Nike's supplier network is structured in two layers (Figure 6.2).

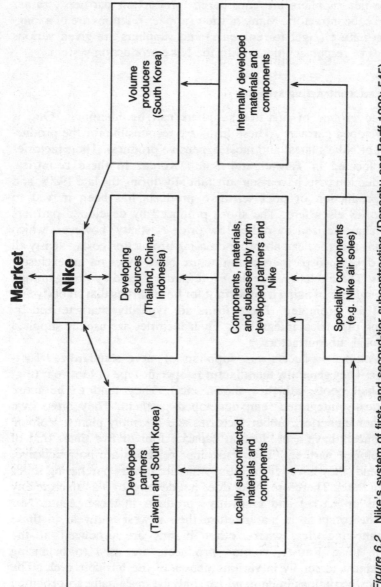

Figure 6.2 Nike's system of first- and second-tier subcontracting (Donaghu and Barff 1990: 545)

The first thing to observe is that Nike's current production system is almost entirely based on out-sourcing to independent suppliers. First-tier suppliers are considered 'production partners', rather than subcontractors. Many of their supplier relations are of a long-term nature (eight to ten years) and suppliers are given various kinds of responsibilities within the Nike production system.

The subcontracting system

Three groups of first-tier suppliers can be identified. One is 'developed partners'. These firms are responsible for the production of Nike's latest and most expensive products. Their factories are located in Taiwan and South Korea. In these countries, production costs have risen substantially during the late 1980s, and so production of price-sensitive products has been moved to factories elsewhere. The shoes produced by developed partners are characterized by rather low price elasticity, however, which means that they can absorb increasing production costs. Nearly all the developed partners manufacture Nike shoes on an exclusive basis. These relations are therefore characterized by strong mutual dependence, making it important for both parties that stability and trust are promoted. These firms are typically characterized by a lack of vertical integration. Their factories are usually supplied by local subcontractors.

'Volume producers' are suppliers of more standardized footwear. They generally manufacture a specific type of footwear (e.g. football boots, athletics shoes, etc.). They tend to be more vertically integrated than developed partners. They often own leather tanneries, rubber factories and assembly plants. Volume producers have a production capacity four or five times that of developed partners. Their customer relations are not exclusive. Instead, they have ten or more separate buyers purchasing shoes from them. Therefore, Nike does not develop or manufacture any of its up-market and innovative products in these plants. Nor do the competitors manufacture their newest footwear in these volume factories, where other brands are produced at the same time. Rather, volume producers are used to balancing demand and supply in various phases of the business cycle. The cyclical variations in demand can only be marginally absorbed by developed partners, owing to their limited capacity.

Consequently, variations in demand can be considerable.

Monthly orders to individual volume producers may fluctuate by 50 per cent or more. Therefore Nike makes only limited efforts to stabilize and deepen its relationships with the volume producers as the strategy is to utilize them for cyclical subcontracting.

The third supplier group is represented by 'developing sources'. Producers in this group are attractive owing to their low costs (especially labour) and their potential to diversify assembly location. Presently these firms are located in Thailand, Indonesia and China. Almost all of the developing sources are exclusive Nike manufacturers. Due to their limited expertise, Nike is very active in assisting these firms in their development. At the beginning of the collaboration, the product and production standard of these firms can be compared to the situation forty years ago in the United States. One important thing for Nike, therefore, is to increase the production capability of these factories to meet the global production standard of Nike. The long-term goal is that a significant proportion of the developing sources over time will become developed partners.

The management of supplier relations

We can see that Nike's supplier network is a mixture of different kinds of relations. Some are long-term while others change from year to year. Some are characterized by deep commitment while others are of an arm's-length nature.

Long-term, intimate partnerships with suppliers must somehow be promoted by customers. Nike uses three main strategies to do this:

1 Nike operates what it calls an 'expatriate programme' wherein Nike expatriate technicians become permanent personnel in the factory producing Nike footwear. While at the factory, they function as liaison between Beaverton's headquarters and R&D to help insure a smooth product development process and maintain quality control.
2 Nike encourages its partners (particularly the older ones) to participate in joint product development activities. Most basic research is performed at Nike's Beaverton facilities, but the responsibility for the development of new footwear is shared with its production partners. The partners are especially important in the search for new material inputs and the

implementation of improved production processes, but these close ties also serve to keep the production partners abreast of the directions Nike intends to take in the marketplace.

3 With those factories that manufacture only Nike products (over half of all the partners), Nike places a monthly order, preventing production from varying more than 20% per month. These efforts to stabilize the production of Nike shoes take place with those factories that have been with Nike for many years as well as with newer producers.

(Donaghu and Barff 1991: 542)

It is interesting to observe the activities undertaken by Nike to increase the capability of their developing sources, but the developed partners also participate in this process. The establishment of developing sources often takes the form of joint ventures between local factories in China or Indonesia and a Nike exclusive developed partner in South Korea or Taiwan, which means that the developed partners have a financial interest in the development of the new sources, and will be interested in transferring their sharing capabilities with these partners.

In this way all three actor groups benefit from deeper cooperation. Developed partners are able to move production of the price-sensitive part of the product programme to locations where cost is lower. They concentrate their own manufacturing activities on the more expensive, image-creating products, where price is less important. Developed partners will also be able to supply developing sources with both components and materials.

Developing sources will clearly be able to benefit from the joint venture. The transfer of various capabilities (from Nike and the developed partner) will accelerate the development of these firms as compared with a situation without these links with the larger network. Advantages will be obtained in terms of manufacturing techniques, owing to the demands from competent customers and the availability of important input resources.

Finally, Nike also stands to benefit from the new structure of the production system. The diversified structure of production hedges against currency fluctuations, tariffs and duties. The joint venture arrangements seem to be an efficient way for a natural transfer of capabilities which must be efficient for the entire network. But the system also keeps the pressure on the developed partners at the first tier. They need to keep production costs low as developing sources might otherwise mature into full-blown developed partners.

Case comments

Nike's way of organizing the production system is an excellent example of a network strategy. It is an extreme case, as the whole production process is out-sourced, but similar tendencies can be found in almost all types of production. Suppliers are becoming more important from a volume point of view, and efficiency is more and more determined by how different production units – internally and externally – are systematically interrelated. In this kind of co-ordination, the activities as well as the resources of the different units must be co-ordinated, and a key issue is to find and develop points of complementarity. For the same reasons, the selection of companies to include in the network is very critical. Nike seems to do this in an excellent way. Their ability to do so is probably attributable to their marketing position in relation to the end market, and to two important knowledge bases. Their position in relation to the end market – the image and the distribution network – is their major asset. In the long run it might not be sufficient, however, and should be supplemented with at least two knowledge bases. The first base is the product knowledge and a need for continuous development regarding individual components, as well as the interaction between different components. This knowledge of how to create good footwear must be kept centrally, in order to keep up the central position within the network. There is always a risk, otherwise, that the developed partners, or the volume producers, might be able to take over. The second base is knowledge of potential suppliers. The development of the production network will never be finalized. There will always be both possibilities of and needs to increase efficiency in terms of finding better activity structures as well as better resources constellations. Every network can, and must, be developed in order to be sustainable.

CONCLUSIONS

Our five case studies have clearly illustrated the potential for increasing efficiency and effectiveness in purchasing activities.

With systematic development of individual supplier relations and supplier networks, significant improvements can be made.

It has also been shown, however, that the potential benefits can be quite difficult to attain. Companies have to change their internal activities, as well as change the suppliers in various ways. Such a process means that a number of critical issues are raised. The major one is that companies need to facilitate co-operation, as their own activities will be increasingly dependent on other actors. For such a division of work to be efficient, two major issues must be dealt with. One is the organization of the companies. Certain types of organizational structures might increase the opportunities for an efficient linking of the actors, activities and resources. Organizational aspects are therefore discussed in Chapter 7.

The other issue is communication. A critical aspect of supplier relations and supplier networks is the exchange of information. As activities undertaken by suppliers are dependent on (and affect) the activities of the customer, there is a strong need for information exchange. Various aspects of this issue are discussed in Chapter 8, which deals with communication in supplier relations and supplier networks.

Chapter 7

Organization of purchasing

In Chapter 2, we began to address the relationship between the organization of a firm and the structure of its purchasing operations. The organizational structure determines the purchasing function, but at the same time changes in purchasing may lead to the necessity of changing the organization. The discussion in Chapter 2 primarily analysed the links between the purchasing organization and the technology and personnel of the firm. The main aspects dealt with were in-house ones, with a particular focus on the balance between centralization and decentralization. The first two sections of this chapter go into further detail on these internal issues in relation both to the organization of the purchasing department and the purchasing function, as well as the integration of purchasing with other internal functions such as production and design. Chapters 4, 5 and 6 have indicated how important individual suppliers and supplier networks are in corporate resource handling. It is thus clear that organizing the firm in a way that facilitates effective exchange with other firms is an important task, and this aspect is examined in greater detail in the third and fourth sections of the present chapter.

ORGANIZATION OF THE PURCHASING DEPARTMENT/ PURCHASING FUNCTION

One classic issue in all organizational structure is the choice between centralization and decentralization. The argument in favour of centralization is that concentration of purchasing can increase the effectiveness of resource utilization. Larger purchasing volumes lead to a stronger negotiating position, which is expected to result in better economic conditions. Larger purchasing volumes also make it possible to use specialized, skilled purchasers with high commercial competence. Making purchasing a centralized function also facilitates the co-ordination of purchasing between the different units of the buying firm and a supplier.

The idea underlying the decentralized purchasing organization is that purchasing is such an integral part of the overall operations of a company that it should not be carried out centrally. This school claims that central purchasing means that the distance between those responsible for acquiring resources and those who work with other functions which affect (and are affected by) these acquisitions becomes too great, and that the purchasing manager must be associated with the other functions as well. This decreases the benefits to be gained from economies of scale, as it means that different units in the company will tend to use different suppliers. This form of organization also leads to purchasers' being less specialized and thus, in one sense, less professional.

Centralization–decentralization

We have already addressed the issue of what consequences the firm's technology (type of manufacturing) and the nature of what is purchased (for example, the difference between equipment and MRO supplies) has in terms of what makes a suitable organizational structure. A third relevant factor is the structure of the network in which the buying firm is one of the actors, and a fourth is the goals of the purchasing firm. These factors include the firm's view of the role of purchasing, whether it should be seen as a cost centre or a strategic acquisition resource, which also has consequences in relation to the status of purchasing in the company. The company's goals will also affect the organizational structure as a whole, with a major impact on the potential of the purchasing department to structure its own organization.

All this means that the choice between centralization and decentralization will always be a compromise. Settling for the benefits of one always means sacrificing the potential benefits of the other. For this reason, purchasing will always have to put effort into eliminating the disadvantages of the organizational form chosen for it. A decentralized purchasing organization may be supplemented with a purchasing staff which draws up group agreements with the purpose of gaining economies of scale. A centralized purchasing organization can be supplemented with shop-floor purchasers who take responsibility for acquisition of specific key components. This makes it possible for most firms to work, in practice, with a combined approach, falling somewhere between the extremes. Depending on where on the scale a firm falls, one may say that it tends towards centralization or decentralization, in its efforts to decrease the disadvantages of the organizational form it has chosen.

Axelsson and Carresjö (1986) and others describe this phenomenon as the pendulum movement of organizational forms. When the pendulum swings too far towards one end of the scale, the disadvantages in terms of centralization or decentralization are so tangible that the organization has to be changed. They discuss one company whose efforts to make its purchasing operations more efficient resulted in a combination of operational decentralization and strategic centralization. This was a mass-production company with many production units, which led to operational decentralization, at the same time as its units had many common suppliers, and its operations were strongly project oriented, with two design units playing a major role, and thus contributing to strategic centralization. The central purchasers worked in various ways, some as product specialists taking advantage of economies of scale by co-ordinating corporate purchasing, some by functioning as division purchasers and actively monitoring purchasing from the perspective of their respective divisions. Some also functioned as project purchasers, with the important task of collecting commercial assessments of projects from an early stage so as to have purchasing options available at the time of tendering. In large companies, the balance between central and local purchasing is particularly complex. ABB (Asea Brown Boveri) has decentralized its purchasing operations. Each company in the group has its own purchasing department, but in order to take advantage of some of the benefits of centralization, ABB has also introduced different types of purchasing co-ordination (see Figure 7.1).

There is one type of co-ordination at the regional level, i.e. nationally. In Sweden, ABB Group Purchasing Co-ordination works with Group Agreements making it possible for the Swedish units to benefit from economies of scale. The various ABB business sectors are also co-ordinated. One of the national companies has been assigned to analyse the potential for co-ordination of the products unique to each business sector. There is a third type of co-ordination at the global level. In these projects,

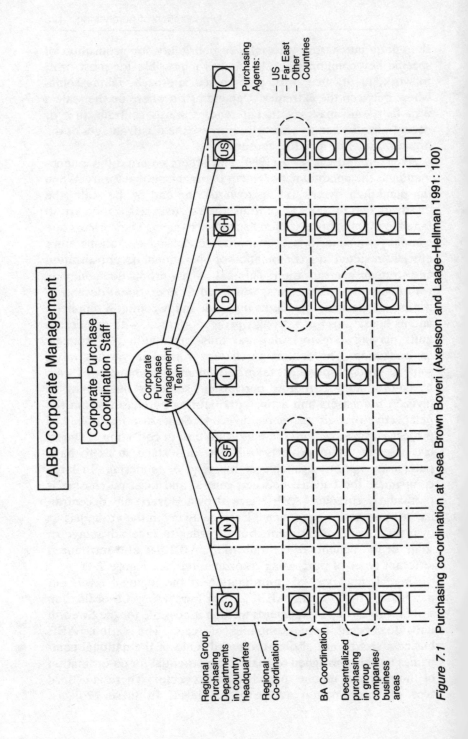

Figure 7.1 Purchasing co-ordination at Asea Brown Boveri (Axelsson and Laage-Hellman 1991: 100)

personnel from different countries work together in efforts to achieve economies of scale for worldwide ABB purchasing. This project works with goods and services used globally in the different business sectors, such as computers, freight, steel, etc. ABB also has a Corporate Purchase Management Team, which works with a fourth type of co-ordination, in which the regional purchasing staff managers meet quarterly to discuss subjects of common interest (Axelsson and Laage-Hellman 1991).

Håkansson and Melin (1978) present other examples of combined efforts which indicate that strategic purchasing issues are not necessarily the best suited to centralization. For example, both raw materials and components can be purchased both centrally and locally. Standardized raw materials and components which could be standardized are well suited to central purchasing, while strategic raw materials and components, vital to production and product design, should be purchased in a decentralized way, in close contact with those responsible for production.

Developments during the 1980s

Naturally, the organization of purchasing is closely tied to general principles of organization. Ericsson (1978) points out how the role and organization of purchasing have changed over time, in step with the total development of the organization of companies. As the 1980s have reflected a general organization trend towards smaller profit centres and more decentralized responsibility, it is natural that advantages of centralization have been seen as less outstanding than in the past, even with regard to purchasing. If purchased components account for a large proportion of total costs, there will be enormous consequences, and not only financial ones, from not allowing independent units to make their own purchasing decisions. If the ambition is to allow individual business units to function as an integrated whole, it is, of course, important to keep the different functions 'close' to one another. One division manager said:

> You can't divide a company up and then say 'We have a central purchasing unit for the whole group.' In that case it also should be possible to concentrate R and D and marketing – damned effective. The only problem is that the whole becomes ineffective because each unit/division loses its effectiveness.
>
> (Melin 1986: 5)

Seen in this light, it is not surprising that the 1980s were marked by the virtual disappearance of the traditional, large purchasing departments. A recent study of large Scandinavian companies showed that only 9 per cent had fully centralized purchasing (Kewenter and Rönnertz 1991). In many cases, central purchasing has been replaced by a purchasing staff responsible for group purchasing co-ordination of common purchases to gain the economies of scale which can, of course, still be won. Purchasing staffs can also be used as service organizations in relation to operative purchasing departments, for example, to supply information on pricing, currency developments, the rate of inflation, and economic forecasts. They may also serve as discussion partners for the purchasing staffs of the individual operative units, and provide specialist expertise (for instance, on legal issues) in major negotiations.

The officials working in this kind of central purchasing unit find themselves working less and less with operational purchasing, and the long-term effect may be decreased professionalism of the purchasing staff. Individuals with a great deal of competence – and interest – in purchasing issues will probably try to work in the operational units instead. This may lead to the purchasing staff's finding it difficult to recruit competent purchasing specialists which, in turn, will probably lead to very little demand for the services of the staff. This sets up a vicious circle, as central purchasing becomes more and more isolated from the operational functions of the company, and the purchasing staff comes to be viewed as the monitoring arm of the executive management, rather than a service organization for the other units of the company. At one company, where the management and purchasing staff moved from offices next to one of the divisions to a separate head office, one of the operational purchasers said: 'Owing to the decentralization, the purchasing staff has become less and less operationally oriented. The move also meant that, geographically, we are further from the operational units, which decreases our staff's ability to be a specialist organization.'

In this firm, there was a very negative attitude towards central staffs. The most common reason for this was the clear policy of decentralization carried out by the executive management. There had been 'a highly conscious effort to transfer decisions, competence and resources out to the decentralized organization' (interview with a representative of the executive management). As this change had been very successful, the units could see no reason for

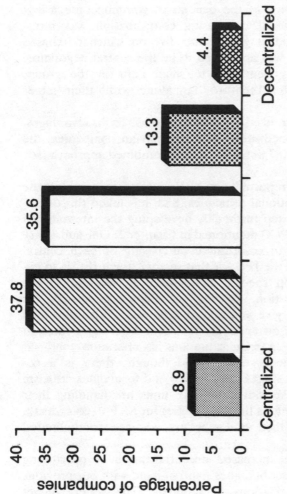

Figure 7.2 Organization of purchasing in big Scandinavian companies (Kewenter and Rönnertz 1991: 43)

■ Completely centralized.

▨ Centralized purchasing of strategic items, decentralized purchasing of commodities.

□ Decentralized purchasing combined with a central purchasing department.

▨ Decentralized purchasing combined with voluntary co-operation between various divisions.

▨ Completely decentralized.

central operations, for example, in terms of purchasing. One purchasing representative interviewed said that, if there is a central purchasing staff, it can be interpreted as a sign of management's lack of confidence in the units. The central purchasing department of this company was later closed down. In order to take advantage of some of the benefits of common purchasing, voluntary inter-divisional purchasing co-ordination was introduced. For each product group, the division which purchased the greatest volumes was appointed to be the central negotiator. This was particularly beneficial to small units in the group, making it possible for them to 'tag along with' their larger colleagues.

But entirely decentralized purchasing also has its disadvantages. In the above-mentioned study of Scandinavian companies, the majority of the firms (87 per cent) used a combined approach (see Figure 7.2, page 129).

We have already reported on ABBs efforts to combine the best of both organizational principles. SKF has taken this organizational model one step further by developing the international purchasing centres (IPCs) mentioned in Chapter 2. One subsidiary has been appointed to co-ordinate purchasing of each central product group (to be the IPC for that sector). Each IPC is to co-ordinate and develop specific competence in relation to the product group in question. As every subsidiary becomes IPC for something, a natural give and take is achieved. Difficulties tend to develop, however, owing to the technical differences amongst the companies, and in crisis situations co-operation tends to fall apart. When the system works, though, there is a co-ordinating unit which reacts to problems and formulates criticism in relation to how the individual SKF units are handling their purchasing. This increases the possibilities for SKF to co-ordinate actions in relation to their vital suppliers, who are strictly limited in number.

The trend towards increased decentralization of purchasing decisions we have described goes hand in hand with our previous finding of changed relations to suppliers. The wider contact interface on which relations are now built is simpler and more natural for a decentralized organization to deal with. What a decentralized organization loses, on the other hand, is a continuous, deep sense of the detailed terms of each supplier market that centralized purchasing functions often had.

ORGANIZATION FOR INTEGRATION WITH OTHER FUNCTIONS

Earlier, we have indicated the need for changed relationships with suppliers to make material flows and production processes more effective. These relationships, however, cannot possibly take place unless the corresponding internal relations also work satisfactorily. In its capacity as an interface to suppliers, purchasing can also serve as a co-ordinator of internal functions.

In a strongly centralized organization, it is difficult for purchasing to play this role, as the sense of 'us' against 'them' easily arises. It is easier, but not without problems, in a more decentralized organization. Factors affecting the possibility of purchasing's playing this type of role will depend on the status of purchasing in the organization, and the relationship between purchasing and other company functions.

Design and development are strongly linked functions. The representatives of purchasing tend to think that it would be possible to raise the effectiveness of a firm's R and D process by involving purchasing from an earlier stage than tends to be the case. Burt and Sukoup (1985) are of the same opinion, claiming that there is a tendency for design to specify components for which there is only one supplier. This leads to problems which could be handled more effectively if purchasing were involved in the process earlier.

Bonoma and Zaltman (1976) show the complexity of this type of involvement, indicating that there are often significant 'cultural' differences amongst the various functions. Designers tend to think of purchasers as overly price sensitive, and as people who are always butting into the business of others. Purchasers often think that designers pay more than necessary for quality, and that their procurement needs to be more effective. The central sphere of conflict is that purchasers want to increase their influence over the process, particularly with regard to specification of what is to be purchased. If the component to be bought is specified in too great detail, the freedom of choice of the purchaser is severely restricted. In order to prevent this, purchasers want to be involved earlier, which designers experience as a threat to their position.

Another cultural factor relevant to the potential of purchasers to function as internal co-ordinators has to do with the status and position of purchasing in the organization. Historically, purchasing has had very low status, as shown by Ericsson (1978), Axelsson and Håkansson (1984) and others. The latter describe purchasing as having developed out of the accounting and inventory operations of companies, and claim that this explains the difficulty purchasing has had in being granted status. Gadde (1989) shows that purchasing managers in one large, divisionalized Swedish company felt held back in the organization owing to their being under the supervision of the production manager. In another case, purchasing felt 'poor response both from the division management and the corporate management', and in a third case purchasing was said to be 'unfortunately, treated as the stepchild in our corporate group'. Corporate management representatives also confirmed the low status of purchasing, expressing the opinion that this led to recruitment problems since purchasing was often considered a department to which people were demoted.

The status of purchasing must be raised to make the important co-ordinating role possible to fill. Kewenter and Rönnertz (1991) claim that there seems to be a positive change under way in this respect. In the study of the purchasing organizations of some fifty large Nordic companies, it was found that in most cases the purchasing manager reported directly to corporate management (Table 7.1).

Table 7.1 Purchasing manager's immediate superior

Immediate superior	Proportion of companies
	%
Managing director	58
Production manager	14
Administrative manager	7
Planning manager	2
Materials manager	17
Project head	2

Source: Kewenter and Rönnertz 1991: 45

These findings imply a substantial rise in the status of the purchasing function. The traditional organizational structure with purchasing subservient to production or material administration was only half as common as reporting directly to the corporate management.

If purchasers are to function as internal co-ordinators, it is also important for existing frictions to be minimized. This can be achieved by reducing the distance between purchasers and other company officials. This distance has a physical dimension – we have already given one example of a central purchasing staff which gradually lost all significance when it was moved from a production unit to the main office. Distance also has a psychological dimension owing to the above-mentioned cultural differences. One way of achieving this reduction is to restructure the organization. Horndahl (1984), for example, has found that the most common way of allocating purchasing work in mechanical engineering industries is for each purchaser to be responsible for one type of product (plastics, sheet metal, etc.), the consequence being that every purchaser is part of a large number of developing projects, and finds it difficult to become involved in any single one, since deeper co-operation would require contact with many designers. According to Horndahl, one alternative would be to use project purchasers who, in principle, would buy all the necessary components for a given development project. This type of project purchaser would have less knowledge of individual supplier markets, as he would have to be familiar with so many, but better knowledge of the demands in terms of production technology. This would probably contribute to reducing cultural differences between designers and technicians. Physical location in the vicinity of one another would make contact more frequent and probably also promote co-operation.

Another alternative, of course, is to recruit purchasers from non-traditional backgrounds. Bergman and Johanson (1978) recommend in this context that purchasers be recruited from the technical core of the company, where they will have acquired the company-specific technical know-how necessary to participate actively in development. Kraljic (1982) is of the same opinion, basing his assessment on a firm which strengthened its purchasing department by hiring an applications engineer with specifically high qualifications. This made it possible to improve the dialogue with design and other technical divisions, and also helped to raise the status of purchasing in the organization. Another company achieved the same effect by hiring purchasers with marketing experience. Such measures may well be combined with active internal marketing of the importance of purchasing to the total effectiveness of the company.

Finally, there is a more radical solution, which is to remove purchasing as a specific position, and to integrate purchasing tasks with others. For example, some construction companies have project engineers who not only deal with purchasing but also with planning and production issues. Since suppliers and subcontractors on many construction projects account for 65 to 75 per cent of the total project, it is easy to see the logic in integrating these functions. Some firms in electronics and mechanical engineering have acted similarly. Integration of purchasing and production has been seen as so central that it has sometimes been demanded that the same person be responsible for both. It is not unlikely that we will be seeing more examples of such organizational solutions, since the amounts of purchased material still seem to be increasing progressively. The need for integration is also affected by the increasing complexity of purchased items. At a seminar, one purchasing director from a large Swedish mechanical engineering firm put forward the opinion that the number of purchasers is largest when a firm's purchasing corresponds to half of its total turnover, after which the number falls. He claimed that this was owing to the need for increased integration with other functions, such as production and/or sales.

ORGANIZING RELATIONSHIPS

Let us go on to discuss organizational aspects in relation to other firms, beginning with organizing individual suppliers and, in a later section, discussing the organizing of supplier networks.

We have already seen that for many companies closer co-operation with individual suppliers is a means of establishing a more effective supply strategy. It is reasonable to think that different ways of organizing purchasing would mean different potential improvements. Purchasing should be important in this respect, owing to the fact that it serves as an interface. In textbooks, purchasing is considered a 'gate-keeper' (i.e. a unit controlling the information flow to a company), which is important in determining which suppliers come into contact with other decision-makers at the purchasing firm.

We base our analysis of organizational issues in an individual relationship on the discussion of supplier relationships presented in Chapter 4. Of course, purchasing firms' relations to their suppliers are very different from case to case. Influential factors previously mentioned include the technological structure of companies and the nature of that which is purchased.

Complexity was mentioned as a characteristic of a relationship.

In complex relationships the number of personal contacts across corporate boundaries may be great. We have previously mentioned that some companies have appointed specific co-ordinators for such supplier relations. The ability of purchasing to play this kind of role will be contingent on what the most critical aspect to benefit from each respective relationship is. If technical aspects are most important it may be difficult, or even unsuitable, for purchasing to play such a role, unless the purchaser is a technician. If commercial aspects are central, the task will be well suited to purchasing. If logistics and material-administrative aspects are dominant, purchasing and production together may be the natural co-ordinators for supplier relations.

This type of co-ordinating function is important in supplier relations, not least owing to the need to match together various officials and activities which take place between the two firms. Moreover, in complex relationships there is always a risk that the supplier will receive different messages from different units and people in the buying company. These messages may be contradictory, and confuse the supplier. If this type of co-ordinating function is to work well, it is important to be clear on which purchasing group has the co-ordinating role and is thus to be seen as the spokesperson of the buyer when dealing with the suppliers. What should not happen is exactly what did happen at General Motors when, in conjunction with an organizational change, a number of different groups were appointed to work with the same or similar development projects. To keep the suppliers from being confused, one of these groups was appointed to be the 'center of excellence' in each project. Nevertheless, one supplier affected by the programme expressed his frustration at finding that all three project groups that were in contact with his firm claimed that they were the center of excellence (Callahan 1986).

The other five dimensions of the relationship, aside from complexity, are the long-term nature, adaptation, trust (rather than formalization), power/dependence and co-operation/conflict. The conclusions of our discussion in Chapter 4 were that closer supplier relations implied longer-term co-operation and a need/ demand for adaptation. This leads to increased dependence, and places demands in terms of increased trust. All this means a shift towards more co-operation in the sixth dimension, but as was emphasized in Chapter 4, it is important to acknowledge the concomitant existence of conflict. The remainder of this section is therefore devoted to a discussion of the first four factors under the heading 'deeper commitment', while co-operation/conflict are dealt with separately.

Deeper commitment

The long-term nature of a relationship and the necessity of adaptability are closely intertwined, as they are both about strengthening the bonds between companies, through reciprocal adaptation and investment. Traditionally, purchasing behaviour has not promoted this type of deeper commitment. Instead, the short-term view and standardization have been the outstanding traits, as part of a conscious effort to avoid dependence. Formalization has been considered more important than trust. Today, when purchasers want to orient their connections more towards long-term relationships and adaptation, many suppliers hesitate, as we have seen. Their previous experience of buying firms' behaviour makes them doubt whether it is wise to make the investments required to fill the new role as system supplier and development resource. The suppliers lack sufficient confidence to establish this new type of connection. Large purchasing firms have worked on eliminating this shortcoming by systematically describing the way their demands have changed and the potential this creates for the individual supplier.

Drozdowski (1985) gives one example from General Motors (GM), where there has been an organizational change made in order to better utilize suppliers as a source of technical development. The first step was to set up a 'New Partnership Program', under the auspices of which, for example, a seminar was arranged at which suppliers were given information about the latest developments in automotive technology and on GM's specific orientation in terms of technical development.

Seminars or other such types of meetings appear to be one means used by many companies for expanding communication with suppliers. The idea is to consider the question of which employees handle relationships with suppliers as an important organizational issue. When the purchasing company tries to alter its relations in the direction of increased openness, it may be difficult for it to succeed and to gain credibility if the same people are used as in the past, when confrontation rather than collaboration may have characterized the relationship. At the same time, it is also difficult to decide immediately which officials should be active in relation to which suppliers. These seminars help create a situation in which various people on both sides can meet and exchange ideas. They also create openings for developing new personal relationships, which may be important elements in future buyer–seller relations.

Occasional activities for expanding the potential for contact in important supplier relations thus becomes a central organizational issue. Another is the development of continuity of commitment. Some officials are very important and active for short periods, for example, in conjunction with a technical development project, while in practice they may be neither motivated nor suitable for longer-term contacts. To date, responsibility for recurring activities in the purchasing firm has, as a rule, been dealt with by individual purchasers or a purchasing team. This is an area where future experience will certainly bring new organizational solutions in its wake.

Co-operation and conflict

The extent to which a given supplier relationship is effective is largely determined by how issues concerning conflict and collaboration are handled. It is an important organizational task to combine individual relationships into the work of the firm as a whole. But relationships also depend on the organizational structure of the supplier, and it must also be taken into account.

Day-to-day work comprises one important dimension of effectiveness. Balance and harmony in both the activity and resource structure are necessary for daily work to function well. Therefore, rationalization of daily activities should focus on minimizing friction in all areas, including technical, administrative and logistic factors, as well as social problems and tension. This can be achieved through close co-operation which, in turn, builds on an understanding of what both companies have in common (purposes, rivals, etc.).

Another important dimension of effectiveness is the long-term nature of a relationship which, in turn, is related to development. The effort to minimize conflict, described above as rational in a short-term perspective, may actually be harmful in the longer range. Suppression of conflict and minimization of friction may lead to a status quo situation which, in turn, poses an obstacle to the necessary further development of the relationship. Development is stimulated by imbalance and problems. An imbalance creates a short-term problem, which disturbs daily routines, but imbalance may also lead to development which may be decisive to the survival of the firm.

In all extensive relationships, it is always possible to make improvements both in the way activities are carried out and the way resources are used. To take advantage of this potential, at least one of the parties must have a sense of 'dissatisfaction'. The organizational stability or harmony desirable to make daily routines run smoothly must, thus, be disturbed by activities (imbalances) which create openings to identify new combinations of resources and/or activities. This makes constructive conflict desirable, provided the organization can deal with it. One of the important tools for this is flexibility, both in terms of how individuals handle situations and how people are combined into groups for handling situations. Relationships must be seen and managed as resources which require maintenance and development. One aspect of this is that each relationship must be seen as part of a larger network.

ORGANIZING SUPPLIER NETWORKS

We have previously seen that any purchasing firm's relations to any given supplier are contingent on other relations. For this reason, organizational aspects of relationships should actually be examined in the light of the total network. Here, however, we have chosen to turn the situation around and not deal with organizational consequences for a supplier network until we have discussed individual relations.

As shown above, the total network of actors and activities can be extremely large, for example, for mass-producing firms in the mechanical engineering industry. The dependence of any firm in the network on others is illustrated by a spokesman for Toyota:

> In order for the Toyota production system to be truly effective, the individual effort of Toyota Motor alone, a mere assembler, would be insufficient. We can approach the completion of the system only when we establish a destiny-sharing community with our satellite suppliers and subcontractors.
>
> (Nishiguchi 1986: 348)

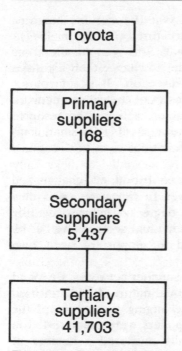

Figure 7.3 Toyota's hierarchical supplier structure (Berry 1982: 25).

Toyota uses a total of more than 40,000 suppliers in its production system (see Figure 7.3). However, only a marginal proportion of these (168) have direct contact with Toyota. The others are organized in a hierarchical structure where primary suppliers are responsible for structuring the rest of the supplier system.

Toyota's production system is one example of a tightly structured supplier network. There is great reciprocal dependence between the purchasing firm and the primary suppliers. As soon as we move to the next link in the chain, interchangeability increases from Toyota's point of view, and it continues to do so throughout the chain, being virtually complete at the far end. This type of system requires a very strong purchasing firm to organize the primary suppliers so tightly and to delegate responsibility to them for the physical flow of materials supply, system supplies and development commitments. It is probably not possible even for a very large, resource-intensive company to organize a supplier structure in this way if its operations are already subject to a different organizational structure. The Toyota system was established from scratch after World War II, when the Japanese automotive industry was entirely restructured (Nishiguchi 1987).

The question is how more 'normal' firms can handle these issues. How can they organize in order to change their identities within the network in the desired direction? It is, of course, possible to adapt to the ongoing processes of change in a network in different ways. Analysis of the actor, activity and resource dimensions in a network should make it possible for small companies, too, to structure their own operations so as to strengthen their identities.

Introducing adaptations may be one contribution to change, and to create space for others to change. In this way, one's own adaptations affect the network. The degree of influence will be conditioned by the strength of the individual actor, as well as by other actors who can be mobilized in support of one's own adaptations.

In our examples of development of supplier networks, we found a number of aspects of an organizational nature. Biopharm tried to reorganize an activity chain by changing the nature of the system used. Some of the major suppliers were uninterested in participating, but Biopharm gradually mustered a number of smaller ones, some of whom were already their suppliers. Not even all the previous suppliers, though, were initially interested, because the scheme disturbed the balance of the existing relationship. Many potential new suppliers did not consider the offer sufficiently interesting. Biopharm eventually succeeded in its efforts to combine in-house resources with individual external relationships and with the network of them, through a combination of active involvement and organization. In one case this led to reorganization of a relationship, replacing contact via an agent with direct contact with the producer. This proved necessary as a result of a change in the nature of the relationship, as it had come to contain more technology.

We also find that Biopharm is a good illustration of how the organization of resource control changed when the buyer became involved in financing (which was a prerequisite for the co-operation) and, in some cases, took over the rights from the supplier.

The example of Volvo uniforms mainly shows how changes in the organization of the activity chain in a network can contribute to increased effectiveness. There were in-house changes at Volvo and at the primary and secondary suppliers, the purpose of which were to improve co-ordination of activities. This also made it possible to make some in-house activities, such as warehousing and production, more effective. A few activities could be eliminated altogether, and others were moved from one actor to another. For this to be possible, changes in the resource structure also had to be made, for example, in the form of equipment for increasing flexibility in inventory handling.

Nike's organization of the supplier network resulted in three different kinds of first-tier suppliers, each with its own specific role and importance. By combining their particular competitive advantages, Nike is able to take advantage of the optimum configuration regarding product development and product quality (developed partners), capacity balance (volume producers) and low cost (developing sources). Another important organizational aspect is joint ventures between developed partners and developing sources, which promote efficiency in division of labour as well as a flow of various capabilities among the actors of the Nike network.

Raising the total competence level in the network was also the driving force for Motorola. The training programme required for suppliers increases the competitiveness of the network as a whole, through an increase in the resource mass. This also leads to improved communication between Motorola and its suppliers, as they gradually come more and more to speak the same language. This type of competence-raising is also a prerequisite for future changes in the activity structure, so that suppliers will be able to take on greater responsibilities.

The Huse–Österberg example from the construction sector illustrates that even a small company can affect its supplier network. Reciprocal adaptations in terms of the structure of product range made it possible for both suppliers and customers to improve their own efficiency. Utilization of the Österberg distribution system contributed to increased co-ordination of the activity chain. For all this to be possible, it was necessary for both parties to see one another as worthy of priority when trying to alter their identities in the network. The measures implemented have led to a tighter linking of activities between the companies, and an increase in the complementary nature of their resources.

One common trait in all the case studies is that, with time, the purchasing firm uses a whole range of tools to affect its suppliers. Therefore, rather than describing the characteristics of the supplier structure in terms of supplier organization, it is more useful to discuss organizing suppliers. The former expression implies a static state, while the latter implies dynamic development. In other words, organizing suppliers is a continuous process in which the purchasing firm is continually striving to develop and combine its utilization of different suppliers.

TOWARDS NEW FORMS OF PURCHASING ORGANIZATION

In summary, the discussion in this chapter has shown that it is necessary to see purchasing organizations in a new way. In the past, organizational structures have mainly been determined by internal aspects. Labour was divided on the basis of specialization of tasks, and purchasing was separated from other functions (production, development, finance). Specialization was then based on the type of product being purchased which, in turn, corresponded to different supplier markets. Monitoring the correctness of purchasing procedures has been a supplementary task for the organization.

The new view of purchasing described here, focusing on supplier relationships and networks, affects the view of what organizational aspects are considered most relevant. Today, companies have to be structured so that different types of activities and activity chains – of which purchasing procedures only comprise a small part – are co-ordinated and made more effective. It must also be possible to handle a number of problems of a technical, administrative, economic and social nature. A number of organizing activities thus have to facilitate pairing with specific counterparts, which means that it must primarily be externally oriented. We have also seen that it is not perfectly clear what shape the new organizational solutions will take, but that certainly the key words will include deeper commitment, co-operation, constructive conflicts and a continual process of reorganization.

Chapter 8

Communication

In Chapter 5, we identified three of the fundamental components of an industrial network – actors, activities and resources. The relations between different activities, and their mutual dependence have already been illustrated. Seen against this background, it becomes obvious that there is need for an exchange of information between the actors and individuals who perform these activities, both within a company and among companies. For example, production activities in one firm are dependent on, and create dependencies with, design activities within the company, supplier activities in the firm from which they purchase, and sales activities at sales level, in the company or with distributors. The effectiveness and benefits of this kind of activity chain are therefore tangibly affected by the effectiveness of the information exchange. This is what makes the communication carried on to achieve this information exchange a central activity in any network.

THE ROLE OF COMMUNICATION IN A NETWORK

In order for activity chains as a whole to function satisfactorily, it is necessary to have information, in anticipation of any activity, of activities already carried out, activities being performed simultaneously, and ones which will be performed later. This information exchange serves to tie activities together, and we refer to it as the co-ordinating role of communication.

Exchange of information and communication are also central in relation to the resource dimension. Different kinds of resources also need to be tied together, as do resources and activities, and actors and resources. Improved communication may result in lower consumption of resources through a decrease in excess consumption, loss, and waste. More effective communication may also enable better utilization of existing resources. More rapid, reliable transfer of information may, for example, make it possible to reduce stock and tied-up capital, by lessening insecurity about fluctuations in supply and demand. This is another dimension of the co-ordinating role of communication.

Information exchange is also necessary to link the actors together. One direct reason for this is the increasing extent to which all activities are split up amongst many actors – this is the trend towards specialization on which we have already touched. The co-ordinating role of communication is therefore also important to the exchange of information between actors.

A second dimension in this respect is related to the need to give other actors the impetus to change in one way or another, for example, to adapt to one another's activity structures. Thus a continuous dialogue is necessary to obtain the necessary reciprocal adaptations discussed above in the section on supplier relations. In this case, communication mostly plays an influential role. This is the second role of communication we identify. It is referred to as the controlling role.

A third aspect of information exchange deals with the transfer of knowledge between buyer and seller. Knowledge of resources and their utilization are decisive to how they can be used. Increasing awareness of a certain resource may give rise to new ways of combining it with other resources, new potential for processing it or for using it in specific activities. Communication about various resources and their attributes is thus very important to their utilization, and communication is thus vital in the increase of knowledge. This role of communication is referred to as the learning role.

In summary, we find that information and communication are essential factors for the effectiveness of an industrial network. We have identified three important roles played by communication in a network: the co-ordinating role, the controlling role and the learning role. It is clear that purchasing serves as one of the main links in this information exchange, as it is the interface of the purchasing firm in relation to suppliers.

This chapter continues with a detailed discussion of communication in purchasing work, and then returns to a discussion of the three roles mentioned above, and the nature of the information exchange. There are also sections on communication in relationships and networks, a focus on computer communication and its future consequences, and a summary.

COMMUNICATION IN PURCHASING WORK

Purchasing activities as such also make substantial demands in terms of information exchange. Some of these demands are in-house ones, resulting from the fact that many purchasing situations involve numerous staff from the purchasing firm in addition to the purchaser. Another aspect of this exchange is external, and has to do with contacts with the selling firm. Here, too, various categories of personnel are involved. Thus the purchasers at a company become important channels of information exchange as well as information-exchange co-ordinators. In other words, communication is, by nature, a vital aspect of purchasing work.

Håkansson and Wootz (1978) found, in one study, that communicative activities (such as telephone calls, meetings and other discussions) occupied nearly two-thirds of the total working time of a purchaser (see Table 8.1). This meant that communication

Table 8.1 Purchasers' activities and contact patterns

Average purchaser activities (as percentage of total working time)	
	%
Telephone conversations	19
Face-to-face conversations	22
Formal meetings	19
Reading, writing, making calculations	28
Miscellaneous work (copying, filing, etc.)	12
	100

Purchaser contact patterns (average percentage of total working time)	
Supplier	21
old	17
new	4
In-house	45
Production division	4
Marketing division	3
Support division (stock, material division, service, etc.)	17
Other purchasers, purchasing manager	9
Other contacts	12
Other work not related to contacts	34
	100

Source: Håkansson and Wootz 1978: 99

was definitely their most dominant working task. In-house communication took more time than external communication, and the relative importance of different types of communication varied greatly. Factors of major impact were found to be the properties of the products, the nature of the supplier markets, and the organizational structure of purchasing.

Information exchange is characterized by considerable variation, partly owing to the features of different types of purchases described above. Purchasing machinery and equipment is characterized by extensive information exchange. Many individuals in the purchasing firm are involved in negotiations of various kinds and thus involve many people in the selling firm and in others as well (consultants, customers, subcontractors, etc.) The frequency of such purchases is not very high, and in many cases there will be no established channels of contact for information exchange. However, this type of transaction leads to the establishment of such channels, as the product will probably be in use for a long time, and will demand regular contacts with the supplier for different kinds of service.

Purchasing components is characterized by a different kind of information exchange, in which the purchasing company has established relations with a supplier for recurring supplies at regular intervals. Achieving precision with regard to volumes and delivery times becomes an important common goal in information exchange between customer and supplier. This type of information exchange may also include more long-term dialogue with regard to technical development of components.

Purchasing MRO supplies is similar to purchasing components in terms of the recurring nature of this type of purchase. However, in contrast with component purchasing, it is more unplanned, and thus more difficult to handle. It is also characterized by the large number of different articles involved, and is therefore characterized by an extensive exchange of information, particularly with regard to orders and payments. As the value of the goods is generally low, indirect costs are relatively very high.

On the basis of this rough survey, we find that there is a great variation in the nature of information exchange. This is related first to differences in purchasing processes with regard to what is purchased, which affects the number of people involved. Each purchasing situation is also characterized by a need to exchange both technical information and more commercial information (about the transaction itself). The time perspective is a third aspect. Every buyer–seller relationship requires communication about the day-to-day exchange, as well as discussion of more long-term strategic issues.

Complexity – and the related uncertainty – is a fourth dimension. Some of this uncertainty must be seen as genuine, as the necessary information is not just difficult, but sometimes impossible, to acquire in advance. One such example is the properties of materials in new applications. The only way of reducing such uncertainty is through tests and joint development projects. Other aspects of information exchange are far less complex. Some are related to inquiries and orders, others to information as to delivery dates. Such uncertainty can be handled by making information exchange between firms more effective.

Seen against the background of these clear differences in the nature of the need for communication, we can see that it is difficult to develop information systems to satisfy all the dimensions of information exchange important to purchasing operations. Some parts can be standardized and routinized, while others can never be structured owing to their characteristics and complexity.

THE ROLES OF COMMUNICATION AND THE NATURE OF INFORMATION EXCHANGE

Information management in a purchasing firm can be classified in different ways. One way, as we implied earlier, is to examine the purpose of communication, identifying the three roles of co-ordination, control and learning.

Another way is to examine the content – the nature – of the information exchange. This may refer to the product – the problem solution – and its attributes, to the commercial terms applying to a purchasing decision, or to the structure of the transaction itself. We may refer to the first as the technical content, the second as the commercial content and the third as the administrative content. There are no sharp boundaries to this classification, which is primarily done for the purpose of identifying some of the typical information needs and making it possible to relate them to the purpose of the communication. After combining the nature of the information exchange with the role of communication, nine types of information exchange can be identified (see Figure 8.1).

Roles of communication	Nature of information content		
	Technical	Commercial	Administrative
Co-ordinating	1	2	3
Controlling	4	5	6
Learning	7	8	9

Figure 8.1 Nine types of information exchange between buyer and seller

When it comes to the technical content of the information exchange, all three roles are of interest. Co-ordination of technical dimensions (1) is a basic prerequisite for functioning interaction between firms. Co-ordination may also refer to the structuring of various activities where technological aspects are central, or to the utilization of resources. For example, it is usually important that the processing of a material at a given stage of the production process is co-ordinated with how the material was processed earlier.

Control (4) is important for the same reasons. By influencing suppliers so that they adapt technically, the purchasing firm may obtain a number of benefits, as discussed above. And, finally, learning plays a corresponding role in relation to the technical content (7). Since relationships are long-term, buyers and sellers will accumulate a great deal of knowledge about one another's technological conditions over time.

Typically, in a business relationship, there is an excess of information and great potential for reciprocal adaptation between the parties. To achieve any lasting effects with regard to control and learning, direct personal contact between the firms is necessary. In both these cases, it is also important to have continuity over time, while co-ordination can be dealt with in a far more standardized way.

The commercial content also contains elements of all three

roles, with the co-ordinating role (2) playing the dominant part. In running activities, there is a need to be able to manage information as to prices, discounts, and terms of delivery and payment. This type of information is necessary for buyers to be able to place their orders.

The learning and controlling roles come into play more periodically. From time to time, the buyer will need more thorough knowledge of the supplier alternatives and commercial terms of the market as a whole. These needs are great, for instance, when equipment and machinery are to be purchased. As these products are bought only seldomly, it is often difficult to even identify potential suppliers. In purchasing raw materials, too, there are substantial needs for knowledge, but of another nature. In these cases suppliers tend to be known, while prices and other conditions may change rapidly. The commercial content and the controlling roles can be exemplified with the need for information in a negotiating situation.

The content of administrative information is coupled to transactions as such. The co-ordinating role (3) is dominant, and the information contains facts about times, volumes, means of delivery, formal roles and routines, etc. When MRO supplies and components are to be purchased, this information content may be the vital element. In purchasing components which are to go straight into a production process, precision in deliveries is central. Exact, rapid delivery information – particularly with regard to deviations from plans – then becomes essential information to the purchaser. In purchasing supplies – often difficult to plan – information as to the ability of the supplier to deliver the goods immediately is important.

All the examples given above are typical of the co-ordinating role. Control (6) and learning (9) are considerably less important with regard to the content of administrative information.

In summary, the need for information is complex both in terms of the purpose of communication and the nature of the information content. This means that high demands are placed on the kind of information exchange in a purchasing firm. Let us go on to discuss different possible solutions to satisfying this need for communication. As in terms of organizational aspects, it is meaningful to distinguish a number of different levels. One is related to the in-house exchange of information in the purchasing firm, another with information exchange in a relationship, and the third with information exchange in a network.

We have also found that some aspects of information exchange appear to be impossible or unsuitable to standardize. The first of these which comes to mind is information related to the technical content and aimed at control or learning (long-term development work). Another relates to parts of the commercial content (such as negotiations). Other aspects, however, such as orders, payments, etc. should be possible to standardize with the aim of mechanizing them and thus gaining rationalization benefits. In terms of Figure 8.1, these characteristics can be found primarily in squares 2 and 3, co-ordination of commercial and administrative information. To some extent squares 8 (learning with regard to commercial information) and square 1 (co-ordination of technical information) may be subject to standardization. It is our opinion that the more complex information exchanges must largely be handled via organizational solutions. The principles of what may promote or obstruct such exchanges were drawn up in Chapter 7.

The remainder of this presentation is, therefore, concentrated on the parts of an information exchange which can be standardized. We also only discuss communication in a relationship and in a network. With regard to in-house standardized communication, we refer the reader to the literature on purchasing systems and their coupling to various material and production control systems.

COMMUNICATION IN A RELATIONSHIP

The exchange of information in a relationship can be made more effective by standardizing the exchanges, for instance, through computer-based communication. This discussion of standardized information exchange is organized in terms of the three dimensions we identified above: technical, commercial and administrative information.

Technical information

The exchange of technical information can primarily be standardized when the purpose of communication is co-ordination. One example is related to the buyer's need of help in problem-solving in a specific purchasing situation. Sometimes a customer needs expert help to choose the specification which will give him optimum performance from items in the standardized product range of the supplier. This may, for example, relate to the choice of size, tensile strength, or rustproofing. To this end, SKF has developed a computerized product catalogue, the CADalogue, providing the customer with recommendations of suggested ball-bearing dimensions, if the customer can specify a number of central parameters for his current needs. Many firms in other industries are working on similar programmes.

Another application may be found at the design and development phase, with regard to components specially adapted to the needs of an individual customer. In such contexts there is frequent transfer of blueprints and other design information between customer and supplier. Computerized transfer is advantageous in this respect both with regard to speed and certainty. Another possibility is for personnel from the customer's firm and the supplier's firm to be able to work simultaneously on the same design project at their CAD terminals. Today, this happens very seldom. In the future it may become more common, and be important in reducing lead times in development work. This approaches the control and learning roles.

Progress in this area is very rapid. One of the companies we studied increased its number of CAD work stations from 25 to 500 in a couple of years, and the number of documents transferred to suppliers annually from 100 to 2,000. There are, however, a few noteworthy problems in utilizing this communication channel. One is of a technical nature, and has to do with the capacity of the telecommunications network. Another is commercial, and touches on problems of integrity. In order to participate in development work, a supplier must be involved four or five years before a new model is presented. Customers in industries where new generations of models are common express some doubts as to how safe suppliers are from a confidentiality point of view. However, this hesitance is hardly related to computer communication as such, but is probably conditioned by the general uncertainty about joint development work.

Administrative information

It was in the context of exchange of administrative information that computer applications were first introduced. One of the most renowned examples of how information technology contributes to raising effectiveness is McKesson Drugs, the American pharmaceuticals wholesaler (see Corey 1985). This firm has an extremely large product range (70,000 articles), and thus it was natural for them to make early use of computer technology to make in-house operations more effective. Moreover, the firm had 92 distribution centres all over the United States, with an enormous total inventory. The computerized information system provided reliable information about current stock volumes at each in-house distribution centre, and the quantities to be delivered by different suppliers during the coming period. Increased accuracy of information made it possible to reduce inventories.

By establishing computer links to both suppliers and customers, it was also possible to improve efficency dramatically in the exchange processes within the distribution system.

Customer information about current and coming delivery potential was also improved once customers were given insight into the inventory system. This resulted in more even order inflow, and also made it possible for customers to cut back their inventory and administrative costs. After eight years (1983) it was possible to show large rationalization gains. The stock turnover rate increased by 50 per cent. The service level – measured as the number of order lines without an out-of-stock note had increased to 96 per cent.

And last but not least, McKesson Drugs' cost structure changed substantially (see Table 8.2).

Table 8.2 Effectiveness impact on McKesson Drugs

	1975	1983
Number of distribution centres	92	56
Number of telephone salespeople	250	15
Number of purchasers	160	13
Customer credit time in days	30	15

Source: Corey 1985

In addition to decreased personnel and inventory costs, it was also possible to reduce the customer credit time. By ensuring customers of delivery the day after they ordered, it became possible for customers to reduce their stocks, which allowed them to accept shorter credit times.

Pappersgruppen, a Swedish paper wholesaler, provides an even earlier example. Their business operations are characterized by a large product range, and a high frequency of transactions with dealers, with a consequent need of frequent contacts and many orders. The computer communication with dealers introduced in the mid 1970s led to effects similar to those at McKesson Drugs. Their stock turnover had doubled by 1981, their degree of service increased from 85 to 95 per cent, and their average customer credit time decreased by half. In this case, these efforts resulted in a redistribution of inventory, and changes in the division of labour among the different actors. For the system as a whole (from producer to printer) inventory was estimated to have been cut back by half, as was capital tied up in credits. The effects for the customer price of the products owing to these reductions were estimated to be almost 10 per cent (Gustavsson and Svensson 1983).

One company in the mechanical engineering industry was able to rationalize its exchange of information as well as its flow of goods through a computer-based communication system established with one of its suppliers (Westling 1986). It purchased MRO supplies very frequently, placing orders many times a day. By introducing a terminal system, orders were transmitted daily with next-day delivery, and invoicing was reduced to once a month (see Figure 8.2). The combination of these measures meant substantial rationalization gains for both customer and supplier.

Commercial information

Commercial information relates to the purchaser's need for information about the commercial terms prior to entering into an agreement. This includes identification of potential suppliers and evaluation of what they have to offer. Originally, expectations were high in relation to this kind of information for computerized purchasing and marketing. Computer technology was expected to provide the purchasing firm with complete information on the supplier structure in different markets and the commercial terms applicable to them in terms of prices, delivery terms, etc. Electronic markets which would make it possible for the purchasing firm to select its suppliers very effectively has been a hot issue.

With experience, these applications have proved to be far less extensive than was expected. Instead, computer communication has proved to be far more important in terms of rationalization of information flows in specific buyer–seller relations. This is, of course, largely attributable to the limited interchangeability of many customer–supplier relations.

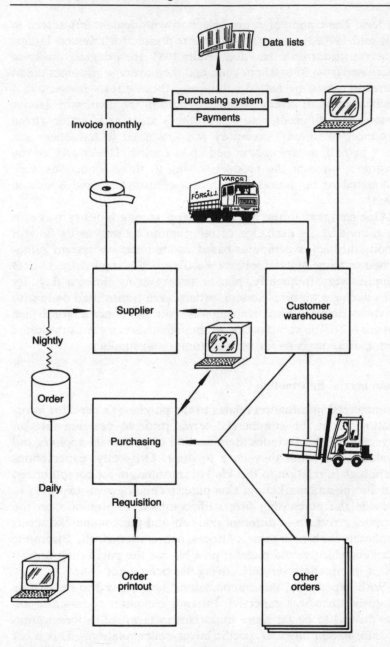

Figure 8.2 Order and delivery system for rationalization of a customer–supplier relation (Westling 1986: 93)

Still, there are a number of systems for handling this type of information on the market. They are product data bases containing various suppliers within one product area. The suppliers connected to the system update their product information and current business terms continually. Such data bases in Sweden include product areas such as building supplies, sanitation, and the restaurant and medical-care sectors.

COMMUNICATION IN NETWORKS

Of the standardized types of information exchange discussed here, computerized solutions have proved to be the most important for exchange of administrative information. For purchasing firms, the systems described offer effective solutions in relation to one supplier. In cases where one supplier dominates (as was the case for McKesson Drugs and Pappersgruppen), such systems may be very useful. For customers who use several large suppliers, they are awkward. With the early systems, the consequence would be that a number of suppliers would have to locate terminals at their customers' firms, since these relationships also needed to be made more effective. Two wholesalers in Sweden, suppliers to the hardware-supplies business (Luna and Järnia) have been pioneers in Sweden in terms of computer communication. However, dealers in this industry use many other suppliers as well, which shows the advantage of having a wholesaler in information exchange – one firm which could couple a number of suppliers with a number of customers. One such system is Bascet Infolink, introduced in the mid-1980s. Six Swedish suppliers were among the founding parties. (Bahco, Atlas Copco, SKF, Coromant (Sandvik) ESAB, and Tibnor). Luna and Järnia joined the system later. In principle, Bascet functions as a computerized switchboard which connects suppliers with customers. As of 1991 roughly 1,200 firms are connected to the system. Less than one hundred of them are suppliers, and the rest are customers.

Similar types of networks have also been established by computer companies. IBM has developed solutions through which a customer and a supplier may be linked up to one another irrespective of what type of computers they use. IBM Information Networks offer a number of services, from electronic mail to more complex systems. For example, IBM may build up a communication system between a firm and its customers and suppliers. This has been done, for example, for the Swedish department store chain of Åhléns. The Åhléns' purchasers enter their orders into Åhléns' mainframe computer, which creates a file to translate these orders to the standardized communications language. The file is transmitted overnight to IBM's electronic mailbox, and then on to the suppliers in the morning. They can then deliver the same day. This has cut back lead times from five days to one.

The number of computerized order systems is growing with time, but a rather limited number of firms are connected up today. Most systems cover a relatively small number of buyers and sellers, and the individual purchasing firm can only communicate with a small proportion of suppliers in this way. Computer firms have made special efforts to supplement their systems with suppliers from the service sector, such as banks and travel agents. IBM

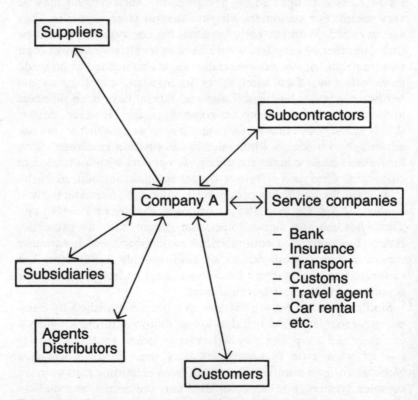

Figure 8.3 Communication network for an individual firm

has developed a number of communication networks for specific firms, as exemplified in Figure 8.3.

More advanced communication networks and complex information exchange systems are used by large purchasing firms in the mechanical engineering industry, who have many suppliers. We have also noted a change of orientation in purchasing operations, leading to increased demands for accuracy in deliveries, both in terms of content and timing. This of course means higher demands being placed on information exchange between customer and supplier. As these firms use many suppliers and combine their components into one production line, standardized communication gives buyers efficiency benefits. During the 1980s, western European automotive manufacturers developed Odette, a joint system for communication with suppliers. The Odette system offers a large number of standardized messages, not all of which are yet in use. One of the main ones is transfer of delivery plans via computer. This was put into use early, and in 1989 Swedish automotive manufacturers transferred more than half of their delivery plans this way. Another important aspect of the Odette system is a standard for marking goods, vital for rationalization gains in transport to buyers.

The Odette system provides one example of EDI information exchange (electronic data interchange). The principle underlying this type of communication is transfer of data files, which means that it does not require on-line connections. (This makes it similar to the IBM Information Network.) Other similar EDI systems are also being developed for other branches of industry, such as CEFIC in the chemicals industry and EDIFICE in electronics. Neither of these is yet as advanced as Odette, however. We can also see that companies outside the branch of industry for which Odette was developed make use of it. For instance Electrolux, the appliance manufacturer, communicates with some of its suppliers via Odette. One reason is that many suppliers serve both Electrolux and the automotive industry.

COMPUTERIZED COMMUNICATION AND ITS CONSEQUENCES

Much of our discussion relating to possible standardization of information exchange in relationships and networks has focused largely on computerized solutions, where major changes are under way today. Some people are of the opinion that computer technology will revolutionize purchasing and marketing. To add depth to the discussion of long-term effects of computerized communication, we go on to discuss the possible effects of this type of solution on total communication in relationships and networks. We also analyse the possible consequences of the changes we have observed on the basic structure of networks, with regard to actors, activities and resources, concluding with comments on the effects on supplier relationships and networks. When we refer to IT (information technology) we use it synonymously with computerized communication.

IT and the communication structure

Up to this point, the potential for computerized information exchange has not much affected communication between customer and supplier. In the study of the British market referred to earlier (Galt and Dale 1991), it was found that only 10 per cent of firms used EDI communication to relate to their suppliers to any great extent; 50 per cent used some aspects of EDI communication to relate to some suppliers, and intended to increase use; 40 per cent had no EDI systems at all, and half of these firms had no plans to establish them.

These findings are not particularly surprising. We saw above that communication accounts for a large part of a purchaser's total time, and comprises highly complex information exchange. This communication is both personal and impersonal (letters, telexes, etc.). Personal contact is used in formal meetings or discussions, either eye to eye or over the phone, and it is improbable that computerized communication will have any decisive effects on this communication range. In the future as well, purchasers will need to exchange information in many ways. As one purchasing manager said:

> We will communicate with some of our suppliers via Odette. Some communicate directly into our computer system. But we will, of course, also use the telephone, telex, telefax and letters where appropriate. Today we send Kanban cards to some of our suppliers, and we will continue to do so.

We will probably be seeing a continued transition towards more rapid, secure media for impersonal communication – from letters and telexes to faxes and computer communication. Clearly, too, the fraction of personal communication which consists of highly standardized information exchange (orders, inquiries, bills of sale, etc.) which often takes place on the telephone today should be transferred to impersonal media. This kind of standardization of routine, operative transaction would give the purchaser more time to deal with more important issues when he speaks with supplier executives, and more time for his own strategic purchasing work such as monitoring trends on supplier markets, initiating and participating in supplier relationships and development projects.

IT and the network structure

We have previously found that, today, many firms are trying to co-ordinate their activities to a far greater extent than previously. JIT deliveries are only one example, but a very good illustration of what can be achieved through improved co-ordination. Higher demands for certainty in delivery plans are also being made, and exact delivery information and systems like Odette can be highly effective. But it is important to note that IT is not a vital prerequisite to achieving this type of communication. The Japanese models of information flow are not primarily computer-based, but built on far more manual handling of paper-based information (Kanban cards).

Although IT is not required to better integrate production activities with those of suppliers, introduction of IT is one way to rationalize information exchange, and is therefore best suited to continually recurring activities. Moreover, development of IT systems can also affect other types of activities. Technical development work is neither repetitive nor routine, but computer communications can still be used in interactive design work. It will probably take time for this type of communication to have a general impact. For the foreseeable future, information technology will be most important in exchange of administrative information.

The situation for the resource structure is different. Earlier in this chapter we found that standardized exchange of information is of very little significance to both the controlling and learning roles of communication. The organization and utilization of the resource structure is a complex process, closely related to knowledge of how various resources should be combined. Owing to this complexity, it is not likely that IT will influence the resource structure to any great extent. One indirect effect is that IT can contribute to freeing resources by improving the effectiveness of the activity structure. Another effect on the resource structure is that the necessary investment in communications equipment to link firms to one another becomes a resource in itself. As we saw when we examined the various solutions, this may strengthen the link either to a specific supplier or to a communications company which ties the actors together. The choice of solution will certainly affect the power and dependence structure in the network.

The solutions in terms of information technology used thus affect the actor structure. We have seen that deepened relations between customer and supplier places demands in terms of reciprocal adaptations, and various investments. Some suppliers do not wish to get involved in such investments, others cannot, because they lack the resources or expertise. Others still may never have the opportunity if the purchasing firms cut back on the number of suppliers they use. But we already know that this is not an effect of IT as such, but rather a consequence of a higher ambition to make better use of one's suppliers, an ambition on which IT has very little impact.

As in all situations of change, some actors will be strengthened and others weakened. It may be of interest in this context to discuss in greater detail who it is that is promoting development of IT. Of course computer and telecommunications companies are central actors. The first major applications were developed in conjunction with distributors, who wanted both to make their relationships with customers more effective, and to strengthen the ties between them. In these cases, IT may be seen as a supplementary means of competition. Other early applications were developed by large purchasers who saw opportunities for a better organization of their complex supplier structures. But we can also see that changes in communication forms make openings for entirely new actors. Computerized switchboards like Bascet Info Link and product data-base companies are two interesting examples of new actors that have developed.

IT and supplier relations

Let us now discuss the effects of computerized communication on some of the main dimensions of relationships and networks.

The complexity of an individual relationship is affected by computerized communication in two ways. It decreases because of the benefits provided by a system that keeps a large number of details in order. It increases owing to new demands for exactitude in deliveries and quality, and it requires new kinds of expertise. Computerized communication may help a large purchasing firm to achieve a great reduction in the complexity of managing a large number of supplier relations, as we saw in the example of the Odette system in the automotive industry. When all suppliers communicate and deliver according to one and the same standardized model, the co-ordinating work of the buyer is greatly facilitated.

However, there is a price tag attached to these co-ordination benefits. Choosing a specific solution such as the Odette system leads to other types of limitations. The Odette system ties the transportation and production systems of the supplier and the customer up with one another (see Figure 8.4). For this type of integration to work well, there must be substantial standardization of both activities and communication. A supplier who delivers through Odette will sometimes have customers in other industries as well. A more general communications solution would make it possible for the supplier to use the same system for these customers as well. The high degree of standardization, however, often makes this more difficult. Another argument for more general solutions is the increasing specialization of the overall division of labour in a network. This development probably means that it will be more and more difficult for individual suppliers to adapt to the highly specialized solutions preferred by their customers.

It is clear that an investment in computer-based communication requires adaptations on both sides, and thus increases the long-term nature of a relationship. One of the main Swedish suppliers to the automotive industry stated in an interview that it was seriously considering the strategic consequences before becoming involved in this type of deeper co-operation.

This also gives us an illustration of the power and dependence dimension. Large purchasing firms can force their suppliers into a system which, in turn, increases the imbalance of their power relations. The development of the Bascet system can probably also be seen as partly caused by a reaction in the power/dependence dimension. The development, promoted by some distributors, was experienced as a threat by some suppliers who represented established product brands. One might see the extension as being a

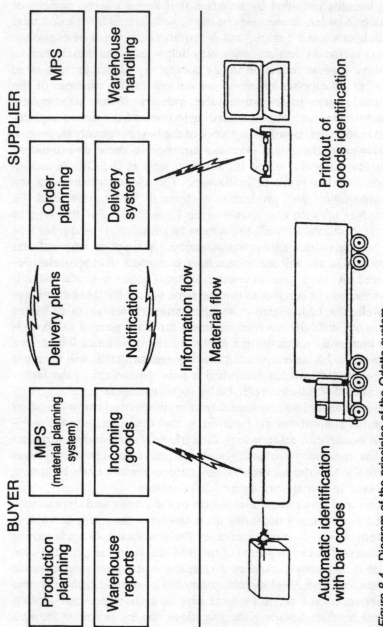

Figure 8.4 Diagram of the principles of the Odette system

situation in which these brands were reduced to article numbers in a wholesaler's order system. Avoiding this vision of the future might have been one of the driving forces for the producers who founded Bascet.

It is also clear that timing will be a central issue in relation to standardization of information exchange. To benefit fully from standardization, all the central actors must be involved. This may lead to postponement of an application owing to a delay in the decision-making process of one of the main actors, for instance about connecting the external communication system to their internal one. For minor actors, becoming connected to this kind of system at the right moment in time may determine whether or not they survive.

COMMUNICATION – A CRITICAL ELEMENT IN ALL PURCHASING WORK

In this chapter, we have argued that communication is one of the key aspects of all purchasing work. To begin with, communication is the essence of all purchasing . Secondly, it plays various roles for the purchasing firm, including co-ordination, control and learning. Thirdly, there is wide variation in information content. The technical content affects the need the product or service will fill both in the short and long term. The commercial content is related to the conditions of doing business, and the administrative content has to do with carrying out the specific transaction. Fourthly and finally, a large number of media are used, although computerized information exchange is the only one we have discussed in any detail.

This does not mean that we see it either as the most important or the best, only that it is the most current in terms of developments in communication. Personal contact is, and is likely to remain, most important. Information technology can also contribute to making personal contact more effective, if the part of the total information exchange that can be standardized (orders, inquiries, etc.) is computerized. This will make it possible for buyers and sellers to take better advantage of their limited time for the more complex types of information exchange which cannot be standardized.

We have described various potential developments in computerized solutions both for individual relationships and networks of suppliers. There is corresponding development potential for other media as well. The greatest potential may be in relation to personal handling of both relations and networks, and developing his personal networks may be the greatest challenge for a purchasing manager today.

In several of the five cases presented in Chapter 6, issues of information exchange and communication proved to be important. In the Huse-Österberg case, co-ordination of administrative information exchange turned out to be vital. It is also clear that the controlling role was an important one. For example, adaptations in the product range were necessary for both parties.

The controlling role was important to Volvo as well, and in that case, too, other parties had to be made to adapt. Rationalization of administrative information exchange was a prerequisite for reducing lot sizes and increasing delivery frequency.

Biopharm is a good example of the controlling role in technical information exchange. There were initial difficulties in interesting suppliers in the necessary adaptations, and the desired effects were only achieved through extensive information exchange.

The Nike and Motorola cases illustrate the learning role. The purpose of the Motorola development programme was to increase the expertise of suppliers through transfer of Motorola-based knowledge. In the case of Nike, knowledge was transferred and shared through active information exchange among the different categories of suppliers.

The last six chapters (Chapters 3 to 8) have analysed purchasing issues from a perspective distinctly different from that of the traditional model for purchasing. The final chapter is devoted to a precise formulation of an alternative model of purchasing which has developed over the last ten years.

Chapter 9

Effectiveness in purchasing

The way we have proposed structuring purchasing problems in this book does not correspond directly with the way purchasing is traditionally analysed. In other words, the view of what comprises effective purchasing work is undergoing a process of change. Doubt is being shed today on methods which were considered effective in the past, and methods which were traditionally rejected are now being accepted. This chapter pursues that discussion and formalizes the conclusions, first by summarizing the arguments developed throughout this book, second by formulating a more explicit and exact alternative model of purchasing, and third by analysing the ways in which it deviates from previously recommended views. We begin by examining the assumptions underlying the classic model, and its consequences. A few selected examples illustrate the discussion, but we also assume that the reader will supplement the analysis with knowledge of the examples from previous chapters.

Let us begin with a discussion of the classic view of purchasing, its effects, and a critical analysis of its basic assumptions, and then go on to present the new model of purchasing, analyse its development potential and conclude with a section of future possibilities.

THE CLASSIC VIEW OF EFFECTIVE PURCHASING

There is a very well-established classic view of how effective purchasing should be carried out (see Figure 9.1). The first step is to specify the needs to be satisfied. The next is to identify a number of suppliers who can deliver a solution which satisfies those needs. They are requested to submit quotations, which are then compared. It is, more or less, taken for granted that it will be relatively easy to decide which alternative will be the best. The differences between the quotations are supposed to be quantifiable, according to some decision rules. The solutions arrived at, however, have often proved that the chosen alternative was the one with the lowest price. Competition between suppliers means that all of them try to keep their costs as low as possible, which is positive for the purchaser. This is referred to as benefiting from the market forces. Effectiveness in purchasing arises when the official responsible for purchasing follows the procedures described above. In other words, the effectiveness is built into the process and, to ensure effective purchasing, it is necessary to monitor that the process is carried out in the prescribed fashion. Purchasers and the purchasing department generally bear responsibility for seeing to it that purchasing follows the established pattern.

1   Recognition of need

2   Description of requirement

3   Selection of possible sources of supply

4   Determination of price and availability

5   Placing the order

6   Follow-up and expediting of the order

7   Checking the invoice

8   Processing discrepancies and rejections

9   Closing completed orders

10   Maintenance of records and files

Figure 9.1   A purchasing decision model (Westing *et al.* 1969: 44)

One of the important underlying assumptions is that independence – or freedom from dependence – leads to effectiveness.

Effectiveness is guaranteed because one party is free at any given moment to select the best partner. Metaphorically, a company may be seen as an island which purchases products produced on other islands, and for which it is possible to change suppliers simply by changing destinations. In other words, the operations of buyers and their suppliers are seen as independent of one another. The effectiveness of the operations of each is also seen as being dependent only on in-house factors, as everyone is considered to have access to the same supplier structure, i.e. the same external effectiveness. Moreover, the cost of coupling the various operations together is limited. In other words, it is not necessary to build bridges when looser connections suffice.

Before the effects of this well-established view are discussed, the assumptions on which it is founded need to be examined. By examining how this view stipulates that buyers and sellers should interrelate, and what revenues and costs are considered relevant, we capture some of its central assumptions.

The relationship between buyer and seller can be described in terms of supply and demand, which must be known and matched. In other words, it is assumed that there are suppliers who can offer the specific product or service demanded by the buyer. This implies in itself that there are other buyers whose needs are identical with those of the company in question. This can also be expressed by saying that there is an established market in which neither the buyer nor the seller is unique.

Another assumption about conditions which can be affected by a company's way of purchasing is how revenues can be increased and/or costs reduced. According to the classic view, interest is completely focused outwards, i.e. directed at the suppliers, with the ambition of exerting price pressure on them by playing competitors off against one another. In a well-functioning market this comparison is 'automatic', which means that purchasing activities are just guarantees that the market mechanisms are working. If the market is not working well, the proposed purchasing process may be seen as an effort to strengthen the market forces.

A third assumption is that price is the relevant cost item to focus on. This is closely related to externally oriented price pressure. The function of the product or service is standardized, as it is offered to and demanded by many companies, and it can therefore be seen as a constant. Furthermore, the buyer's own in-house costs in conjunction with the purchase are seen as independent of, and therefore not susceptible to influence from, the choice of supplier. This makes price the only item which can be influenced at the time of purchasing, and it also means that price variations reflect only the costs or mark-up of the supplier. Thus lower prices are always to be preferred.

EFFECTS OF THE CLASSIC VIEW

Application of the classic view has various effects. Some are intentional and others are undesirable. The description below deals with the main effects, concentrating on the negative ones, and neglecting the positive, desirable ones, since the changes in purchasing work that have taken place in many companies in the last twenty years have mainly aimed to reduce these negative effects.

The first effect can be illustrated with a piece of advice traditionally given to all purchasers: 'Buy as close to the source, i.e. as far back in the processing chain, as possible!' Intermediaries are seen as price padders, and purchasing directly from the manufacturer is seen as a means of price reduction. The effect of this is that the purchasing organization takes over a large number of handling and warehousing activities, performing for itself the product-range and service functions which could be dealt with by intermediaries. The number of suppliers with which the purchasing organization is in contact increases, and the volume per supplier decreases. The purchasing structure is fragmented, and the purchaser has to serve an important co-ordinating function. Looking at the structure at a higher level, we find that this means that every unit has to deal with overall co-ordination, which results in high costs and a great deal of complexity.

Another effect is that suppliers are seen as dangerous to approach, since proximity creates dependence, while independence is the desirable state. In other words, suppliers must be kept at arm's length, so they can be exchanged at any moment in time. Freedom, independence, takes this central position when dependence is seen as a market flaw which, by definition, inflicts higher prices on the buyer. In other words, dependence is seen as resulting in increased costs.

A third effect of the classic model of purchasing is that suppliers are always seen as interchangeable. If a supplying company fails or behaves badly, it will be immediately replaced. In Hirschman's terms (1970) the sanction 'exit', or non-purchase is used. But the supplier has a way of rebounding immediately, which is to offer a lower price in the next round. Correspondingly, a supplier who behaves well is not 'rewarded'. Rather, the supplier has to compete on the same grounds in the next round as well. Every situation and transaction are judged (at least mainly) in isolation.

There is a fourth effect, which affects suppliers. To be competitive, i.e. to keep prices down, they have to reduce their own costs as far as possible. They therefore implement internal efficiency measures in terms of production, administration, and goods handling including packaging and transport. Such changes are also good for the buyer, provided they do not lead to increases in in-house costs. However, this is often exactly what happens, as changes in the suppliers' routines may directly affect the in-house functions of the purchasing firm.

A fifth effect is that interplay between buyer and supplier mostly focuses on the problem of division. Negotiations with the supplier are thought of as being about his mark-up or profits, and price discussions become discussions about the division of profits. The buyer's profit is the supplier's loss, and vice versa. The result of this is that far too little energy is invested in finding new and better solutions.

A sixth and final effect is that the classic model of purchasing leads to high transaction costs, illustrated in the following example from the construction field. When a library was to be built in southern Sweden, thirty quotations were submitted. The costs associated with producing these tenders, for these thirty contractors and their subcontractors, had to be covered somehow – i.e. they had to be paid for by some buyer. In twenty-nine of these thirty cases, they had to be covered by a different buyer from the one on whose behalf the cost was incurred. As this procedure is frequently repeated, all buyers end up doing some of the paying, sooner or later.

The example above indicates some of the effects of the classic model of purchasing. In the last two decades, an increasing number of purchasing firms and organizations have judged the negative effects as altogether too great, and they have therefore gradually altered their purchasing behaviour. Different companies have changed in different ways, as the examples in this book have shown. By compiling and reviewing such observations, we can identify an alternative model for purchasing. Before describing it, let us analyse the objections to the classic view, by re-examining the basic assumptions on which it is founded.

CRITICAL ANALYSIS OF BASIC ASSUMPTIONS

The classic view of effectiveness in purchasing is based on three assumptions. In the section describing the classic view above, we identified them as homogeneity of supply and demand, price pressure on suppliers and considering price the main cost item. Below, we examine them from last to first, beginning with the assumption that price is the most relevant cost item. It has gradually become evident that price does not primarily reflect the more or less given production conditions from the buyer's point of view but rather the entire functional relationship between buyer and supplier, which means that it also reflects the behaviour of the purchasing firm. Let us examine this in greater detail by analysing how the cost of a product (or service) is established, step by step, using a cost scale. The example in Figure 9.2 allows us to follow a product from its manufacturer via a distributor until it comes into use by a buyer. The product follows a flow chart through the three participants, successively tying up resources, i.e. incurring costs.

Some costs arise with the manufacturer, others with the distributor and others still with the user. When the product has ultimately been consumed, it has also reached its end cost or total cost. A cost scale makes it possible to visualize the dependence amongst activities, and the consequent costs to the different units. If the

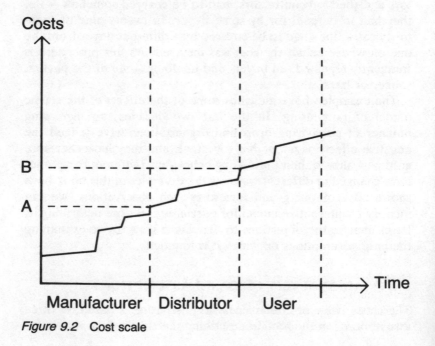

Figure 9.2   Cost scale

user buys in one way, demands one type of delivery, product design, delivery time or service, all this will have cost effects for the manufacturer and the distributor. The cost scale also illustrates the way in which every activity has its price, and that its magnitude varies depending on which party performs the activity. It also indicates that activities are often duplicated unnecessarily, for example, when the last thing one party does is to test the product, and the first thing the next one does is to test it again.

The cost scale also provides an excellent illustration of the potential of the user for reducing his stock (and thus decreasing the time, tied-up capital and storage associated with a product) without the manufacturer or distributor having to make corresponding increases in these areas. Provided that planning and ordering routines are developed, the whole flow can be made more effective, and the 'end cost' reduced, despite the fact that prices A and B might have to be adjusted upwards. Thus these prices are to be seen as reflections of how the chain is organized, how activities are distributed, rather than as external conditions, impossible to affect.

In light of all this, it is justifiable to question the validity of the assumption that price is always the cost item which needs to be minimized. Instead, price should be considered a result of the organization of the chain of refinement, and seen in relation to the costs and benefits in other dimensions of using a given supplier.

The second basic assumption was that outwardly oriented price pressure was the relevant variable for increasing the effectiveness of purchasing. Many firms have now found that there are a number of ways of using their means of purchasing to affect their in-house costs. For example, it is possible to reduce in-house production and materials-handling costs dramatically by collaborating more closely with suppliers. This is also true of administrative costs and benefits as well as the costs associated with development projects. Joint development also affects the revenues of the buyer. Purchasing can thus be seen to impact on the total revenues and cost structure of the purchasing firm, which can also expand its own activities, both developing them and making them more effective, by broadening its view of purchasing. JIT deliveries is only one example of available means.

The third assumption was of supply and demands as givens. In this respect, too, doubt has been cast on the classic view. The existing supply should not be seen as a given but rather as something which can and must be affected and developed by the buyer, who must actively influence the suppliers. Large companies have begun to take this view for granted, and even local and national governments have begun to be active in this area, for example, when they procure technological equipment. The interplay between supply and demand – the dialogue between buyer and seller – has grown more direct. This means that a different working method is required of purchasing from the one promoted by the classic model. Although the size of the purchasing firm impacts on its ability to affect suppliers, the examples we have given in previous chapters show that small buyers can also have substantial effects if their efforts are aimed at the right type of partner.

FORMULATING AN ALTERNATIVE MODEL

In principle, the alternative view of purchasing operates on the assumption that no parameters in the relationship between buyer and seller are to be taken as given, that everything is open to impact. Information and close contacts are, however, required in order for any impact to take place. What this means is that buyer and seller 'invest' in one another, and grow closer. One result of this is that it becomes more difficult for the buyer to play suppliers off against one another. The established supplier knows very well that the buying firm has also invested in their relationship, and that the investment will be lost if the buyer changes supplier. Under these circumstances, cost pressure must be created by other means, although the threat of a future break, the option of each unit to choose partners independently still remains important. Both parties enter into the relationship voluntarily. So, at least in the short term, cost pressure must be created within the individual relationship. This places increased demands on how individual relationships are handled, with the consequence that purchasing work becomes more difficult and more important. It is more difficult because solutions to problems in various dimensions – technical, material handling and commercial – are required, and it becomes more important because to some extent the automatic market mechanisms are thrown out of joint and have to be replaced with other more directly oriented cost-pressure measures. A simple model helps us to see more exactly how the new model for purchasing works in comparison with the old one from an economic point of view:

$$V_i = R_i - TC_i \quad \text{in which}$$

V_i = the value generated when supplier i is used
R_i = the revenue improvement in various dimensions created for the purchasing firm by supplier i
TC_i = the total cost of using supplier i.

This means that the value of using a supplier is equal to all the positive effects minus the negative ones (the costs). The cost item can also be divided into two, external and in-house costs, i.e.

$$TC_i = EC_i + IC_i \quad \text{in which}$$

EC_i = costs paid externally (price + freight, insurance, etc.)
IC_i = purchasing costs which arise in-house in relation to handling the supplier, i.e. costs for negotiation, contacts, invoice handling, etc.

This makes the total expression

$$V_i = R_i - EC_i - IC_i$$

According to the classic model, in principle R_i and IC_i are constants, and equal for all conceivable suppliers. In practice, it is recommended that existing differences are to be evened out before a decision to purchase is made. What remains of the expression is

$$V_i = K - EC_i \quad \text{in which K is a constant.}$$

In this case, the highest value of V is obtained when EC is lowest. In other words, the lowest price gives this highest value.

According to the alternative view, all three variables are seen as important variables and also as interdependent. It is particularly emphasized that R_i varies greatly, which is what makes it a variable worthy of primary attention. But the interdependence among these three variables means that they must be judged and assessed within the same context.

Let us begin by examining them one by one. R_i is a complex item containing all the advantages with which a supplier can provide a buyer, in the form of added revenue. Various examples have been presented in previous chapters. One important aspect of this item is that products can be improved through development co-operation and quality assurance. Cost savings in relation to materials handling (the buyer's in-house transport, storage, etc.), tied-up capital, production and technical development are other aspects of this item, as are cost reductions when the product is used (such as maintenance) and when it is phased out (discarded or scrapped). In other words, various conditions are likely to be affected by the behaviour of the supplier, and the benefits accruing from this behaviour in the form of extra revenue (reduced costs) should be referred back to the supplier.

We have previously established that both parties' learning more about one another is a prerequisite for being able to achieve this increased revenue. Thus R_i is directly related to investing in the relationship. It is through the joint and reciprocal learning generated in the relationship that potential arises for increasing revenues. One thing which further complicates the picture is the fact that the value is also contingent on how the particular relationship is intertwined with others, i.e. its place in a network. In other words, the value of R_i can be written as

$$R_i = f \text{ (Relation }_i\text{'s connections to the company network)}$$

and in order to increase R_i, investment is necessary. The revenue generated must, then, be set off against the increased costs of the relationship in question.

The second variable in our total model, EC_i, requires no detailed treatment here, as it has been so thoroughly analysed elsewhere. It might be added that price should be seen as an indicator of the cost scale presented in Figure 9.2. And it should also be pointed out that price is still important – as in many cases it accounts for a substantial part of the total cost item.

The third variable, IC_i, does require further comment, however, both because it is related to R_i and because it has received special attention at some companies. Application of the classic model has led, in many cases, to such a fragmented picture of purchasing that purchasing costs such as supplier contacts, invoice handling, etc. have taken on such proportions that they require special efforts. We have presented examples of this in relation to the construction sector and its extensive work with invoice handling and monitoring. Another example is the city of Stockholm, where most procurement is local, but which still had 15,000 suppliers in 1986. For these reasons, some firms 'reward' their purchasing managers for reducing the number of suppliers and/or invoices. The purpose of doing this is, of course, to reduce unnecessary administrative work and to make room for more positive work through investments in relationships, which increases R_i.

Thus the item of IC includes costs for systems common to all suppliers and costs for handling individual suppliers. The latter can be further subdivided into a running and a more investment-oriented part. One main difficulty is that when contacts deepen, it becomes more and more difficult to draw the boundary between costs specific to one relationship and running costs for production, development, and even sales. This applies to the R_i item as well.

On the whole, we find that items R_i and IC_i are difficult to measure exactly in their entirety. What is easier is to measure and specify changes in the R_i and IC_i items when efforts are made to change them. For example, it is possible to estimate what the magnitude of cost changes and effectiveness benefits of using five suppliers rather than sixty would be.

Looking back on the total model and comparing the classic view of purchasing with the alternative one, we find that focusing interest on pricing restricts the space for action with regard to other facts which impact on costs and revenues, and thus also limits the potential for benefits in effectiveness. The advantage of the classic model is its simplicity with regard to recommendations, follow-up and performance. Tackling the entire V_i factor in collaboration with suppliers, pursuant to the alternative model, creates far greater potential for rationalization benefits and development work. But there are also disincentives, including the fact that a purchasing department becomes as difficult to evaluate as are development, organizational or marketing departments. The increased demands for integration with production and development will probably also mean that purchasing is less and less often handled in a separate department.

PROBLEMS WITH THE ALTERNATIVE MODEL

There are also a number of problems and risks associated with the kind of purchasing work described here. One risk mentioned in Chapter 3 may arise if purchasing and supplier issues are separated from the rest of the company's in-house operations. As we have said, JIT is not only a philosophy meant to characterize supplier relationships. Essentially, it is a production philosophy. This is also true of quality and development issues in supplier relations.

Of course all these aspects must be built into the overall in-house operations of a company and, moreover, they must also be built into the company's customer relationships.

Another risk – always present when new ideas are to be applied – is associated with too rapid or too extensive involvement in the use of sophisticated supplier relationships. If this happens, the company may have trouble keeping pace with the changes, adapt too slowly, and be unable to utilize the available potential. Special competence is also necessary to be able to promote relationships effectively, and such competence takes time to build up.

There is a more problematic risk associated with the balance between implementing measures and decisions in the short and the long term. Finding the balance between utilizing that which has already been developed and building up something new also poses problems. Some aspects of a deeper commitment to a relationship can best be satisfied by geographical and cultural proximity to the supplier, while others can best be satisfied by large multinationals with advanced research and development programmes. Finding this balance in terms of capability for a company also becomes an important long-term issue. This also means that building up relationships with these suppliers is an important task, at least for large companies, since the supplier network becomes a power factor. It may, therefore, be important in the long run to give priority to a less competent more local supplier, even when there are more competent suppliers elsewhere. There is, of course, no universal solution, no best or only way. The risk is that short-term aims will take the upper hand and, instead of building up relationships, companies will invest in utilizing what they already have. This may be harmless to a company in a wealthy environment with many potential suppliers, such as Silicon Valley, but harmful if this is not the case. Thus supplier development becomes an extremely important strategic issue.

There is one additional, more structural, risk for small buyers with regard to availability of suppliers. Since different suppliers become linked to certain demanding buying firms, they are likely to be less and less interested in new customers, especially if those are small. We may then anticipate demands for more active efforts from purchasing firms to involve their suppliers and awaken their interest in collaboration. In other words, we anticipate an industrial structure in which purchasers will have to be considerably more active and more demanding than they are today.

DEVELOPMENT POTENTIAL

During the 1980s, the transition from the classic view of purchasing to the alternative one, described above, has revolutionized some companies. The effects that have been seen have not only influenced their ways of thinking, but also their continued behaviour. These companies appear to have had vast potential for improvement and, despite all the changes made, most of them still seem to feel that they have just taken the very first steps in a development process. This is natural, as they have only begun to seek out and utilize all the possible combinations in linkings to different suppliers. Until the early 1980s, most corporate executives seem to have been preoccupied with examining the possible internal combinations, with the production manager as the natural driving force. Production and marketing issues were also dominant in the work done by boards of directors, and purchasing is still seldom a topic on the agenda at board meetings. Systematic analysis of the supplier structure is even less an issue for top management, but a gradual change in this view is sure to take place. By expanding the strategic analysis and including different possible relationships with suppliers, the total development potential of a company increases remarkably. There are possible combinations in a number of dimensions, including technical functions or properties, administration, materials handling, transport of goods, communications, etc. Just as a company not only can but must develop its in-house effectiveness, it must also go on continually promoting relationships with suppliers.

Not all companies have yet seen or utilized the development potential of purchasing, as can be seen in Table 9.1, which shows the number of technical development relationships a selection of small and medium-sized Swedish production firms have with their suppliers.

Table 9.1 Development relationships with suppliers

Number of development projects with suppliers (during the past 3 years)	Proportion of firms %
0	27
1–2	22
3–5	35
6–9	8
10 or more	8

Source: Håkansson 1989: 78

As can be seen in the table, more than one-fourth of the firms was not pursuing any technical development work with a single supplier, half were with two or less, and 85 per cent had a maximum of five development relationships with their suppliers. Since, for the group of companies investigated, purchasing accounts for an average of 50 per cent of their turnover, there is clearly potential for development. Of course there is great variation as to what kind of development projects are needed, depending on the type of business involved, but there is no question that there is always potential for development. A reasonable forecast for the 1990s is that matters relating to supplier relationships will be considered important to both productivity and development capacity.

The development expected will have a clear impact on suppliers as well. Companies will be encountering more and more buyers who both have higher demands and who are more interested than in the past in having proposals for special solutions. In light of this, selling firms will probably need to work on their ability to react, and to respond to different customer demands, instead of developing solutions of their own and then trying to market them.

Bibliography

Abernathy, W. and Clark, K. (1982), 'Notes on a Trip to Japan'. Graduate School of Business Administration, Harvard University, Boston.

Asplund, E. and Wootz, B. (1986), 'En inköpsstrategisk omorientering', *Purchasing Magazine*, No 1, 60–4.

Axelsson, B. and Carresjö, U. (1986), 'Inköp som spindeln i nätet – om utveckling av inköps roll vid Ericsson Radio Systems', *Purchasing Magazine*, No 2, 14–22.

Axelsson, B. and Håkansson, H. (1979), *Wikmanshyttans uppgång och fall*. Studentlitteratur, Lund.

Axelsson, B. and Håkansson, H. (1984), *Inköp för konkurrenskraft*. Liber, Stockholm.

Axelsson, B. and Laage-Hellman, J. (1991), *Inköp – en ledningsfråga*. Mekanförbundets förlag, Stockholm.

Bergman, B. and Johanson, J. (1978), 'Inköp och produktutveckling', in Inköp, Håkansson, H. and Melin, L. (eds). Norstedts, Stockholm.

Berry, B. (1982), 'Is Detroit Prompting a Shake-Out in the Supplier Network', *Iron Age*, 14 July, 25–8.

Blenkhorn, D. and Noori, H. (1990), 'What it takes to Supply Japanese OEMs', *Industrial Marketing Management*, 19, 21–30.

Blois, K. (1971), 'Vertical Quasi-Integration', *Journal of Industrial Economics*, Vol. 20, No. 3, 33–41.

Bonoma, T. and Zaltman, G. (1976), 'Organizational Buying Behaviour'. Proceedings of Workshop on Industrial Marketing, University of Pittsburg.

Börsveckan (1989) 'Kapitalbindningen i svenska börsföretag', No. 13, 3–4.

Burt, D. (1989), 'Managing Suppliers Up to Speed', *Harvard Business Review*, July–August, 127–135.

Burt, D. and Sukoup, W. (1985), 'Purchasing's Role in New Product Development', *Harvard Business Review*, September–October, 90–7.

Callahan, J. (1986), 'Cost Cutting, Confusion Plagues GM', *Automotive Industries*, August, 27.

Cayer, S. (1988), 'World Class Suppliers Don't Grow on Trees', *Purchasing*, 25 August, 45–49.

Cook, K. and Emerson, R. (1978), 'Power, Equity and Commitment in Exchange Networks', *American Sociological Review*, Vol. 43, October, 721–39.

Corey R. (1985), 'The Role of Information/Communications Technology in Industrial Distribution'. Working Paper, Harvard Business School, Boston.

Culliton, J. (1942), 'Make or Buy', Graduate School of Business Administration. Harvard University, Boston.

Dagens Industri (1988), 'Inköpskungarna i bil-Sverige', 22 December, 10–13.

Dillforce, W. (1986), 'Purchasing – A Singular Way to Increase Competitiveness', *Financial Times*, 24 October.

Dion P., Banting, P. and Hasey, L. (1990), 'The Impact of JIT on Industrial Markets', *Industrial Marketing Management*, 19, 41–46.

Dirrheimer, M. and Hübner, T. (1983), 'Vertical Integration and Performance in the Automotive Industry'. Paper presented at the Future of Automobile Forum, MIT, Boston.

Donaghu, M. and Barff, R. (1990), 'Nike Just Did It: International Subcontracting and Flexibility in Athletic Footwear Production', *Regional Studies*, Vol. 24.6, 537–552.

Drozdowski, T. (1985), 'Purchasing at GM Restyles for the 90s', *Purchasing*, 24 October, 56–60.

Dubois, A., Gadde, L-E. and Håkansson, H. (1989), 'The Impact of Information Technology on Purchasing Behaviour and Supplier Markets'. Working Paper No. 1989: 11. Institute for Management of Innovation and Technology, Gothenburg.

Ericsson, D. (1978), 'Inköp och räntabilitet', *Ekonomen*, No. 5, 6–9.

Eriksson, A-K (1989), 'Teknisk utveckling i leverantörsnätverk – Biopharmfallet'. Working paper, Department of Business Administration, Uppsala University.

Eriksson, A-K. and Håkansson H. (1990), 'Getting Innovations Out of Supplier Networks'. Paper presented at the conference Networks of Innovators, Université de Quebec, Montreal.

Gadde, L-E. (1978), *Efterfrågevariationer i vertikala marknadssystem*. Business Administration Studies, Gothenburg.

Gadde, L-E. (1989), 'Inköpsfunktionens utveckling till strategisk konkurrensfaktor – förändring med förhinder'. Chalmers Tekniska Högskola, Institutionen för Industriell Organisation och Ekonomi.

Gadde, L-E. and Grant, B. (1984), 'Quasi-integration, Supplier Networks and Technological Cooperation in the Automotive Industry.' Proceedings from International Research Seminar on Industrial Marketing. Stockholm School of Economics.

Galt, J. and Dale, B. (1991), 'Supplier Development: A British Case Study', *International Journal of Purchasing and Materials Management*, winter, 16–22.

Gemünden, H.G. (1985), 'Coping with Inter-Organizational Conflicts. Efficient Interaction Strategies for Buyer and Seller Organizations', *Journal of Business Research*, Vol. 13, 405–420.

Gilbert, J. (1990), 'The State of JIT Implementation and Development in the USA', *International Journal of Production Research*, Vol. 28, No. 6, 1099–1109.

Grant, B. (1990), 'Inköpsstrategi och organisation i stora verkstadsföretag'. Institute for Management of Innovation and Technology, Gothenburg.

Gustafsson, B. and Svensson, R. (1983), 'Distributionsekonomi och kapitalrationalisering', *Marknadstekniskt Centrum*, Skrift 21. Liber, Malmö.

Håkansson, H. (ed.) (1982), *International Marketing and Purchasing of Industrial Goods – an interaction approach*. John Wiley and Sons, Chichester.

Håkansson, H. (ed.) (1987), 'Industrial Technological Development. A Network Approach', Croom Helm, Beckenham.

Håkansson, H. (1989), *Corporate Technological Behaviour – co-operation and networks*. Routledge, London.

Håkansson, H. and Johanson, J. (1985), 'A Model of Industrial Networks'. Working Paper, Department of Business Administration, Uppsala University.

Håkansson, H. and Melin, L. (eds) (1978), *Inköp*. Norstedts, Stockholm.

Håkansson, H. and Wootz, B. (1975), *Företags inköpsbeteende*. Studentlitteratur, Lund.

Håkansson, H. and Wootz, B. (1978), 'Effektivt inköpsarbete', in *Inköp*, Håkansson, H. and Melin, L. (eds). Norstedts, Stockholm.

Håkansson, H. and Wootz, B. (1984), 'Låga priser eller låga kostnader?' *Purchasing Magazine*, No. 2, 83–84.

Hägg, I. and Johansson, J. (eds) (1982), *Företag i nätverk. Ny syn på konkurrenskraft*. SNS, Stockholm.

Hammarkvist, K-O., Håkansson, H. and Mattson, L-G. (1982), *Marknadsföring för konkurrenskraft*. Liber, Malmö.

Harbour, J. (1986), 'What is Just-In-Time Manufacturing', *Automotive Industries*, January, 14.

Hay, E. (1988), 'It Takes more than Low Bid to be World Class', *Purchasing*, 10 November, 50–80.

Hayes, R. and Abernathy, W. (1980), 'Managing Our Way to Economic Decline', *Harvard Business Review*, July–August, 67–77.

Helper, S. (1986), 'Supplier Relations And Technical Progress: Theory and Application to the Auto Industry'. Department of Economics, Harvard University.

Helper, S. (1989), 'Changing Supplier Relationships in the United States: Results of survey research'. IMVP International Policy Forum. MIT, Boston.

Hervey, R. (1982), 'Preliminary Observation on Manufacturer–Supplier Relations in the Japanese Automotive Industry'. The Joint US-Japan Automotive Study. Working Paper series No. 5. University of Michigan, Ann Arbour.

Hirschman, A.O. (1970), *Exit, Voice and Loyalty*. Harvard University Press, Cambridge, Mass.

Horndahl, B. (1984), 'Inköpsfunktionens roll i företagets produktutveckling', STU-rapport 82–5890. *Styrelsen för Teknisk Utveckling*, Stockholm.

Hutchins, D. (1986), 'Having a Hard Time with Just-In-Time', *Fortune*, June, 56–58.

Ikeda, M. (1987), 'An International Comparision of Subcontracting Systems in the Automotive Component Manufacturing Industry'. First Policy Forum, International Motor Vehicle Program, MIT, Boston.

Janch, L. and Wilson, H. (1979), 'A Strategic Perspective for Make or Buy Decisions', *Long Range Planning*, Vol. 12, December, 56–61.

Jansson, H. (1982), *Interfirm Linkages in a Developing Economy – The Case of Swedish Firms in India*. Acta Universitatis Upsaliensis Oeconomiae Negotiorum, 14, Uppsala.

Johanson, J. (1982), 'Production Technology and User-Supplier Interaction,' in *International Marketing and Purchasing of Industrial Goods*, Håkansson, H. (ed.). John Wiley and Sons, Chichester.

Kewenter, J. and Rönnertz, S. (1991), 'Analys av inköpsstrategier i större nordiska industriföretag'. Chalmers University of Technology, Department of Industrial Management, Gothenburg.

Klint, M. (1985), *Mot en konjunkturanpassad kundstrategi*. Department of Business Administration, University of Uppsala.

Kraljic, P. (1982), 'Purchasing must Become Supply Management'. *Harvard Business Review*, September–October, 109–117.

Kumpe, T. and Bolwijn, P. (1988), 'Manufacturing: The New Case for Vertical Integration', *Harvard Business Review*, March–April, 75–81.

Lamming, R. (1989), 'The International Automotive Components Industry: The Next "Best Practice" for Suppliers'. IMVP International Policy Forum, MIT, Boston.

Leenders, M. and Nollet, J. (1984), 'The Grey Zone in Make or Buy', *Journal of Purchasing and Materials Management*, Fall, 10–15.

Marier, D. (1989), 'The Post Japanese Model of Automotive Component Supply: Selective North American Case Studies'. IMVP International Policy Forum, MIT, Boston.

Melin, L. (1986), 'Strategiska val för inköp', *Purchasing Magazine*, No. 2, 4–12.

Miles, R. and Snow, C. (1986), 'Organizations: New Concepts for New Forms', *California Management Review*, Vol. XXVIII, No. 3, 62–73.

Morgan, I. (1987): 'The Purchasing Revolution', *The McKinsey Quarterly*, Spring, 49–55.

Newman, R. (1988), 'Single Source Qualification', *Journal of Purchasing and Materials Management*, Summer, 10–17.

Newman R. and Rhee A. (1990), 'A Case Study of NUMMI and Its Suppliers', *Journal of Purchasing and Materials Management*, Fall, 15–20.

Nishiguchi, T. (1986), 'Strategic dualism: A Japanese Alternative'. Unpublished Ph.D. thesis draft.

Nishiguchi, T. (1987), 'Competing Systems of Automotive Components Supply: An Examination of the Japanese "Clustered Control" Model and the "Alps" Structure'. First Policy Forum, International Motor Vehicle Program, MIT, Boston.

Nishiguchi, T. (1989), 'Is JIT really JIT?'. IMVP International Policy Forum. MIT, Boston.

Puto, C., Patton, W. and King, R. (1985), 'Risk Handling Strategies in Industrial Vendor Selection Decisions', *Journal of Marketing*, Vol. 49, Winter, 89–98.

Raia, E. (1988), 'JIT in Detroit', *Purchasing*, September 15, 68–77.
Raia, E. (1991), 'Taking Time Out of Product Design', *Purchasing*, April 4, 36–39.
Roos, L-U. (1988), 'Kapitalrationalisering i varulager – kan japansk management och japansk syn på inköp utnyttjas?' Handelshögskolan i Göteborg, Företagsekonomiska institutionen.
Spekman, R. (1988), 'Strategic Supplier Selection: Understanding Long-Term Buyer Relationships', *Business Horizons*, July–August, 75–81.
Stundza, T. (1985), 'Chrysler: The Purchasing Story that Hasn't Yet Been Told', *Purchasing*, 25 July, 42–49.
Takeuchi, H. and Nonaka, I. (1986), 'The New New-Product Development Game', *Harvard Business Review*, January–February, 137–146.
Westing, J., Fine I. and Zenz, G. (1969), *Purchasing Management, Materials in Motion*. John Wiley and Sons, New York.
Westling, K. (1986), 'Datorkommunikation för effektivare inköp', *Purchasing Magazine*, No. 2, 92–93.
Womack, J., Jones, D. and Roos, D. (1990), *The Machine that Changed the World*. Macmillan Publishing Company, New York.
Woodward, J. (1965), *Industrial Organisation – Behaviour and Control*. Oxford University Press, London.
Zipkin, P. (1991), 'Does Manufacturing need a JIT Revolution', *Harvard Business Review*, January–February, 40–50.

Index